Piotr Adamowicz
Andrzej Drzycimski
Adam Kinaszewski

GDAŃSK

ACCORDING TO
LECH WAŁĘSA

Gdańsk 2008

When I was a boy, I associated Gdańsk with a big city
with a harbour and shipyards. I knew it was the place where
World War II began. I had also heard that Gdańsk had
a lot of historical monuments. That was as much
as I knew back then.

In the late spring of 1967, I got on a train and left
for the seaside.

I got off at the Gdańsk Main Railway Station. A moment
later, I met a friend from back home who talked me into
working at the Shipyard. It was in Gdańsk that I met my
wife Danuta, it was here that our children were born...
And so I became a Gdańsker by choice.

Today, after many years, when I have got to know many
cities in Europe and throughout the world, I can say that
I would never swap Gdańsk for any New York, Paris,
Brussels, Tokyo or Moscow.

Towards the end of the 20th century, Poland gave Europe
and the world Pope John Paul II. Gdańsk, in turn, gave
its country, but also Europe and the world, Solidarity.
Nothing greater could happen to us, the contemporaries,
and to our posterity.

Lech Wałęsa 31 August 1980.

Gdańsk according to Lech Wałęsa

When walking along the Royal Route in Gdańsk, you walk along Długa St., take snapshots at Neptune's Fountain and then cross under the Green Gate to the River Motława – you can be sure that you're taking part in a quite extraordinary historical spectacle.

The Green Gate is the historical home of the Kings of Poland during their stays in Gdańsk, and today it is also the workplace of a Nobel Peace Prize laureate, former President of the Republic of Poland, the leader of the non-violent Solidarity revolution, the former chairman of the largest trade union on Earth.

It is there, at a broad desk, on the second floor from the arch of the Gate, with an excellent view of the entire stretch of the Royal Route, all the way to the Golden Gate, and from the other side over the River Motława and Granary Island, that you can find Lech Wałęsa's office.

View of the Green Gate and a panorama of the Gdańsk Main Town with the Long Market and the Main Town Hall. The Green Gate's top floor houses L. Wałęsa's office.

Few people have the opportunity to look upon the achievements – and the failures – of their lives from such a vaunted vantage point. It is a kind of privilege and gift of fate.

But Wałęsa's story is also our story: the history of Poland in recent decades. He is a living Gdańsk history lesson for his fellow Poles: how we ourselves have changed, our standards, our notions about the world, our struggle, independence and justice.

The two most important lessons which Gdańsk gave to Poland were December 1970, with its bloody confrontation between the shipyard workers of the Coast, the "industrial working class," as it was known back then, with the communist authorities;

Monument in Westerplatte, on the site where the Second World War began on 1 September 1939. Its form is reminiscent of a chipped bayonet plunged into the ground. Unveiled in 1966. Its designers are Adam Haupt, Franciszek Duszeńko and Henryk Kitowski. John Paul II met here with the youth of Poland in June 1987.

and August 1980: a universal lesson, with global consequences – the victorious Solidarity revolution, which closed the chapter on Soviet dominance in Central and Eastern Europe. And which opened the chapter of the independent Polish Republic, unified Germany, the collapse of the USSR, the rise of the independent Baltic States and Ukraine, an entire chain of political changes.

All this happened in Gdańsk. Recently.

When one looks through Lech Wałęsa's office windows in the opposite direction, one sees a view of the River Motława, a waterway which leads to the Gdańsk Shipyard and to Westerplatte, where the Second World War began, where also quite recently the Polish Pope spoke to us:

Every one of you young people finds their own Westerplatte in their lives, some dimension of challenges which you must take up and meet. Some order of laws and values, which must be maintained and protected. Defended for yourselves and for others (...). [JDBN]

And so there is a lot to ponder, when sitting at the desk in the Green Gate...

Let us, however, leave former President Lech Wałęsa at his computer for a while, where through the internet he leads an animated dialogue with the current events in Polish and global politics, where he plays a never ending "match with the rest of the world." Today, these internet debates fill in for his earlier rallies at factories, halls and stadiums. Here he accepts salutes from around the world and from his compatriots; at times he has been mocked here as well. Let us get back then to everyday Gdańsk, the place where we live day in and day out, where one day a young boy from a godforsaken village in the Kuyavia region came...

This is Gdańsk according to Lech Wałęsa.

Gdańsk, which for him was not a place of tourist attractions, but first and foremost a place which forced him to answer the basic questions which history posed.

So how did it all begin? Fifty years ago...

Lech Wałęsa (second row, second from right) on a school trip. Primary school.

The beach in Gdańsk-Jelitkowo

I left Popowo for the first time some time after I graduated from primary school. There's an exact date on our class photo on the beach in Gdańsk: 2 June 1958. [DN]

Ten years later, the village of Popowo: direction Gdańsk

The years went by, Wałęsa worked at POM (Powiatowy Ośrodek Maszynowy – County Machine Centre), and had the reputation of being the best handyman around: he repaired not just harrows but also motorcycles and television sets, washing machines even. He would stand the boys a bottle of vodka at parties, he could afford it... a heartbreak might happen...

(...) I wasn't doing anything important, I was wasting my time, too long. I was already 24 years old. And then came that afternoon. (...) I came home; I didn't want to say that I was making a big decision, I wasn't sure of it myself. So I just said that I was going somewhere to get some fresh air. I took my money, my coat and went to the train station in Dobrzyń.

So, why did I come to the Coast? I thought then that I was going there because the train was most convenient, the next one was to Gdynia through Gdańsk. But that's not how it is with decisions, now I understand this more clearly.

There was the sea, the memory of the school trip of something vast, open, of freedom. And a big city, a seaport, adventure. The choice was subconscious; driven by instinct, like an eel, I felt that there, in this big population centre, was the source of my strength, that I would find myself there or dissolve there. [DN]

Four decades in a man's life is enough to look back with the proper perspective. Forty years ago Wałęsa came to a city whose spirit and history have a clear message: bravery, justice and prudence...

During the memorable strike of 1980, one could feel the motto from the thousand-year-old city's coat of arms – *Neither Rashness nor Timidity*, in other words "With Courage, but also with Prudence" – linger in the air like an obligation. Did the strike leader and electrician Lech Wałęsa ever read those words?

When he stood at Gate No. 2 and spoke to the participants in the event which came to be called historic, it seemed to everyone that these words carried the weight of not only Gdańsk, but also Biblical meanings.

In any event, he can now talk about this to students in Leicester, where Keith Vaz, an enterprising member of the British parliament, who organised Wałęsa's visit to England, took him to his constituency:

Come to Gdańsk. Gdańsk is a nice city, it was built by people of many nationalities over its history (...), it's a multinational city as regards its culture and its achievements, so you can find everything there. [FD]

Next day in London, at Parliament, Wałęsa delivered a short, evocative lecture about geopolitics from the Polish point of view, interrupted by animated reactions from the audience – applause and laughter:

As you know, Poland lies between Russia and Germany.
These nations were fond of tourism. They would visit each
other... and of course the shortest way was through Poland...
and when they would enter Poland they found that it was
a nice country and decided to stay for a while. Once they even
decided to stay for over one hundred and twenty years.
We were wiped off the map of Europe, wiped off the map
of the Earth. Most recently, after World War II,
it was the Soviets who moved in. For over fifty years.
I'm telling you this because nations who experience such
things are quicker to sense certain processes and often warn
the world about threats and opportunities (...). [FD]

Gdańsk Main Railroad
Station. It was here in 1967
that Lech Wałęsa got off the train
and became a shipyard worker
by profession and a Gdańsker
by choice.

From an electrician at the POM plant
and the Popowo marshlands...
A road not unlike that in an American movie

There are many important places in the Gdańsk chapter
of Wałęsa's biography: first Gdańsk, the Shipyard, the
Gdańsk districts of Stogi and Zaspa, but right after that
Warsaw, Rome, Washington, London and Tokyo. Many
capitals and cities throughout the world.

Main Gdańsk Railway Station, Doki St. – Gdańsk
Shipyard. Shipyard Worker's Number 61,878

Gdańsk's shipbuilding traditions date back to the
Middle Ages. Even today we still have the medieval
name of the Lastadia district (for lastage, or the lading
of a ship). By the 17th century many men-of-war
of the Polish Navy were built in Gdańsk.

The traditions of the Gdańsk Shipyard, where the young
Wałęsa found work, date back to the Klawitter,
Imperial and Schichau shipyards of the turn
of the 19th and 20th centuries.

The Schichau Shipyard manufactured the German U-boats which evoke ominous associations of their destructive effectiveness in World War II – associations not without a tone of professional respect.

After the War, Gdańsk Shipyard was established in its stead, and in it the coal-ore carrier Sołdek was built: the first post-war Polish vessel, on which Polish shipbuilders and engineers learnt the difficult art of shipbuilding.

I came to Gdańsk Shipyard three times in my life.
I first applied for a job there on 30 May 1967, right after arriving in Gdańsk. I went there by chance.
I had just got off the platform when the train left the station and before I even had a chance to look around, I met my friend Tadeusz from vocational school in Lipno. It turned out that he had worked in the Shipyard for several years and he advised me to do the same. When I came to the recruitment office and went through the entire procedure I got my Shipyard Worker's Number 61,878 and began work in Department W-4. [DN]

Twenty-four-year-old Wałęsa came to the largest factory on the Polish coast, which then employed sixteen thousand people from all over Poland, and would later expand even more. It was a Tower of Babel, although it was the locals, the Kashubians, who still remembered the pre-war shipbuilding traditions, who set the tone. The engineering personnel were often veterans of the interbellum COP (the Central Industrial District), but there were also Gdańsk University of Technology graduates. The Shipyard was the apple in the eye of the region's party authorities; every launch with the presence of government representatives meant a potential promotion. The communist secret services also kept a close watch, first the *Urząd Bezpieczeństwa* (Office of Security), then, after it renamed itself, the *Służba Bezpieczeństwa* (Security Service). A lot of different things can happen in such a melting pot...

Gdańsk Shipyard, Department W-4 (Equipment)

The first time I came to the Shipyard in 1967, I felt terribly lost. Me, the handyman from POM! After all those years amongst the old jalopies I would dismantle to the last screw, as a guy who likes to know how things work, I was a good repairman. But when I came to the Department and then when they took me on a ship for the first time, when I got lost on a couple of floors of the scaffolding in the cargo hold and couldn't find the exit – I could feel that I was only one of the many thousands there. It was an unpleasant feeling, but I couldn't turn back, I hate turning back. (...) First I went to work in Mosiński's team. This was a team of electricians who wired fishing vessels. Wiring 60 metres of cable as thick as a man's forearm from the generator to the main board, with a difference of levels of up to 60 metres, wasn't an easy matter. The cable had to have the right elbows, the right bends, the right drainage and it couldn't be either too long or too short: it had to be just right. We would first stretch it out on land, taking it off the cylinders, placing it provisionally, estimating the number of elbows, bends, bypasses, etc. If someone made a mistake and it turned out that at the end of our day's work the cable was too short – it was a disaster. You couldn't lengthen a cable. [DN]

**Shipyard lodgings: Klonowicza St.,
hotel in Tuwima St., 28 Kartuska St.**

The Shipyard's workers' hostels and the lodgings
for workers incoming from throughout Poland newly
employed in Gdańsk Shipyard were an extension
of communist Poland's landscape and the lifestyle
of the "industrial working class." They were
simultaneously a confirmation and, paradoxically,
a contradiction of the socialist dogma. Eighteen
hundred people from the hostels and two thousand from
the lodgings would go to work at the Shipyard from
there every day at six o'clock in the morning.

The Shipyard lodgings and hostels varied greatly.

*The worst place was the workers' hostel in Klonowicza
Street. A large complex of five-storey houses standing
together, with six hundred inhabitants, it was an enormous
community. There was a porter's box with a gate – one
entered as if into a camp, to the courtyard. There was nothing
there, just burnt-out grass and dumped bottles. After each
pay day there was vodka, girls coming through the porter's
box just like that, (...) twelve doors broken. A guy was closed
up with his girlfriend and then his mate would come in and
kick the door open (...) Living there was impossible, you could
only sleep over there or get drunk.*

*One of the houses in Klonowicza was a house for families
where I came to live when I married Danuta.*

*The workers' hostel in Tuwima St. was somewhat different,
as the young people there took care of their rooms. You'd have
a picture hanging on the wall, a calendar, straw ornaments.
You never saw that sort of thing in Klonowicza. If someone
managed to endure the stress of the job and the stress of living
in a place like that, they would look for lodgings in the city
on their own after a while. A guy would talk someone into*

sharing a room. The owner of the flat would get money from the Shipyard and the guys would often pay on top of that. It still came out cheaper than living alone. And they would live in a civilised way. That was the first sign that a guy was legit. (...)

My first lodgings as a shipyard worker, where I lived as a bachelor with three mates, was a small room at Mr and Mrs Król's flat in 28 Kartuska Street. I lived there for over two years until I got married. The flat was on the ground floor of an old townhouse and the windows of our room with four beds and a table in the middle faced a busy street with a tram passing by. It was no luxury accommodation, but the owners created a family-like atmosphere and we all liked it. It was close to the Shipyard and to the city centre. We helped them in their household chores, we'd wash the floors on Saturday, sometimes whitewash the walls, sometimes fix something electric; we would even go out to parties with the Króls' eldest daughter. As chaperones. Mrs Król's husband, who I would address as "Guv," was an old-fashioned pre-war agronomist and we would often spend entire afternoons talking politics. He would religiously listen to Radio Free Europe and he reminded me of my stepfather. His payback for my calling him "Guv" was to call me "Leader" and that's the way it remained between us until he died.

The townhouse in Kartuska neighboured a building which was well known and feared in Gdańsk, as it was where the District Office of Security was based. The secret policemen who worked there lived in the nearby houses, including one above the flat where I lived with my mates. Years later, I met the same man in a completely different role as one the minders who would stick to me when I was released from internment. He was one of those who would follow my every step, follow me to and from work, when I went for a weekend holiday, when I would go fishing or to the forest. [DN]

Wartka St. by the River
Motława, in the centre
the Kubicki Restaurant
which dates back to
the pre-World War II period.
In communist Poland one
could pay for a sumptuous
dinner at Kubicki's with
Shipyard work cards.
Photograph from 1950.

Gdańsk after hours, late 1960s

Work at the Shipyard was not easy. At quitting time
Wałęsa closed the cubby-hole where his electrician's
workshop was at directly across from what was then
Gate No. 3. Rare afternoons were spent getting to know
the city and its customs. His mates would more often
frequent the Shipyard bars: Pod Kasztanami (Chestnut)
or Pod Kaprem (Privateer). When there was money
to spend, it would be Kubicki's. In those days you could
pay for a sumptuous dinner with vodka for the entire
company at Kubicki's with Shipyard work cards.
This was Shipyard currency, accepted from everyone
from the Shipyard. A waiter, when he had such cards,
would ask another shipyard worker, "I've got a job
for twenty-five hundred zlotys, want it?" And a patron,
if he wanted to work a bit on the side and earn some
more, would buy it.

*(...) I felt lonely in Gdańsk and when a bright face with
hazel eyes and long hair in a plait looked at me from a flower
kiosk, I remembered that provocative but gently girlish
gesture for a long time. After a few days I came by again and
straight away asked when she was off and closed the kiosk.
She lived at her aunt's in Brzeźno and had come to Gdańsk
from a small village at the same time I had. Her name was
Mirka, but I preferred her second name Danuta.* [DN]

Świerczewskiego (now Nowe Ogrody) St.

The story from the other side of the window
of the Orchidea flower kiosk, across from the Regional
Hospital, late afternoon, 14 October 1968. The future
Danuta Wałęsa was eighteen years old then.

*I liked him. He came to change some money and was
in a big hurry. It all began when he borrowed a book from
me and gave it back after a couple of days. I don't remember
the title. I was about to leave and he asked if he could
walk me home. First we would go to the movies every day,
for maybe a month, then we got bored with that. I went
with him to speedway matches a couple of times. We arrived
at the following daily schedule: he would go to work
at the Shipyard at six, after work he would come to me,
we would talk for a few minutes, then he would go to his flat
in Kartuska Street, went to sleep, come for me before six,
waited for me to close the flower shop and then we would
go for a walk.* [DN]

The honeymoon: Malczewskiego St. in Siedlce district, Beethovena St. in Suchanino district, by the 115 line bus stop, hostel in Klonowicza St.

She

*We were married on 8 November (1969), and four years
later Leszek arranged for the Shipyard to get us a flat
– a small room in Malczewskiego St. (in the Gdańsk
district of Siedlce). We lived there until April 1970.
The landlady was a mean-spirited, nosy woman. She rented
us a connecting room where there was only a cretonne
curtain instead of glazing in the door. (...) Then we moved
to the attic of a detached house in Beethovena Street.
The conditions there were very primitive. That was where
Bogdan was born, just before December 1970; after a year
we moved to a worker's hostel in Klonowicza St.* [DN]

He

I pondered over it only when they played me the wedding march. When we came from our wedding, we were in fact high and dry: I had to leave my bachelor's shipyard lodgings, we had no home or money. And so we were forced to wander from one flat to the next; cold, incidental places where we left part of our life. In Beethovena St. (in Suchanino) we moved into a flat above a hairdresser's run by a lady repatriated from the former eastern territories, which belonged to Poland before World War II. In 1956, she received a primitive house as compensation for the property she left behind in the USSR. She lived there and worked as a hairdresser, raising her son as a single parent. We tried to help her out somehow; just like us, she didn't know anyone here so I was the witness at her teenage son's confirmation, and Danuta helped out in the garden. I would pick up the shovel as well: the plot in Beethovena St. reminded me of my home. [DN]

Gdańsk Shipyard becomes the Lenin Shipyard

The same address, the same shipyard... Gdańsk Shipyard, already known throughout the world and building quite good vessels which were listed in Lloyd's Register, changed its name overnight, against all principles of good commercial practice, to the Lenin Shipyard in Gdańsk. [DN]

This was the initiative of the Shipyard's director Piasecki, who – although previously promoted by the opinion-forming Polityka weekly as a new model western style "socialist manager" – fell into disfavour with Comrade Gomułka, the First Secretary of the Polish United Workers' Party (PZPR), who was suspicious of any novelties or departures from the style he himself adhered to. In an interview, Piasecki had boasted of his high salary, love of luxury and yachting. And then, when a new vessel built in the Shipyard was launched, Piasecki was ignored... No one important

from the Party authorities came to the Shipyard.
And then the director proposed adding "Lenin"
to the Shipyard's name. Such a celebration could not
be missed by anyone. A big cast of Vladimir Ilyich
Lenin accompanied the sessions of the Inter-Factory
Strike Committee in the Shipyard's BHP Hall[1].
The paradox of history.

Gdańsk – the lesson of December '70

The Shipyard would greet the heroes of socialist labour,
Socialist Youth Union newsletters hung in the Shipyard
Departments' wall display cases, but the dogma
about the leadership of the Party and the leading role
of the working class cut both ways...

Already well over a dozen thousand strong,
the shipbuilders were a real force, dangerous
to the authorities. And the Shipyard people knew
their strength...

On Saturday, 12 December 1970, Party officials
went round the Shipyard Departments and read
the letter of the PZPR Politburo to Party members
about the announced general price rise. A discussion
was supposed to follow. There was no discussion;
the strike began.

---

[1] The BHP Hall was a building at the Shipyard allocated for industrial health
and safety training as well as all important meetings concerning the staff.

The burning building of the Voivodship Committee of the Polish United Workers' Party in Gdańsk. A helicopter flies above, with the Shipyard cranes in the background. 15 December 1970.

Gdańsk Shipyard, Management Building

(...) A couple of us went up to the management, including me. We went to the director and stood at the window, so everyone standing downstairs could see and hear us. The Director asks, "What is it you want?" Since I knew the matter and knew what we wanted I asked whether the Director could help set free the workers who were arrested when they went to the Voivodship (Regional) Party Committee the day before and whether he could repeal the new prices of food. The Director replied that he could neither repeal the prices nor set free the arrested. When I asked again whether he could take care of these two demands we had, he said no.

They had a speaking tube there. I announced through the tube what I had heard a moment before. "What shall we do now?" I asked. And the people standing in front of the Management Building downstairs shouted, "Let's go!"

The rallying cry caught on and slowly the people set off. [DN]

"Everyone has their own Westerplatte..."

It seems that Lech Wałęsa had two Westerplattes in his lifetime. The first he lost, though it gave him the bitter fuel of memories and experiences to last a lifetime. And then there was his second Westerplatte: the victorious Solidarity revolution.

The first was in December 1970, when the Shipyard workers marched into town in protest of the price rises, and Wałęsa – as usual – not even knowing how it happened, was in the first ranks. People would later say, "December was like Kronstadt[2]," as they could not find better words to describe the scale and the drama of those events...

[2] The scene of an anti-Bolshevik uprising brutally put down by the Red Army in 1921

Hanging wreaths on the Shipyard wall after 1 May 1970. The person in the foreground is hammering a nail upon which the wreath will hang.

The day was 15 December 1970, the stage was first the Shipyard Departments, then at the rally at the Management Building and in the Director's office. Then the action moved to the centre of Gdańsk, from Doki St., at the Shipyard's Gate No. 2, where the Monument to the Fallen Shipyard Workers now stands, to the former Regional Committee of the PZPR (near the Gdańsk Main Railway Station) – which was where the authorities were at. And finally, to the junction of Świerczewskiego (now Nowe Ogrody) and 3 Maja Streets. This is where the City Police Headquarters was as well as the prison where the shipyard workers who had protested earlier were detained.

For Wałęsa, December's lesson of rebellion, humiliation and bloody threatening experience began at the Shipyard:

I slammed the door (of Director Żaczek's office) shut. I ran downstairs. I caught up with two guys at Gate No. 2. I ran on and caught up with the crowd. I got out in front. I simply overtook everyone. Right next to the Shipyard was the PKS (state coach company) repair shop. I managed to get well up in front, some five metres in front of the crowd. I looked and saw policemen running in our direction. There must have been about thirty of them. They had their truncheons raised. I didn't have anything so I thought I was going to get beat up for sure. After all, I couldn't turn back now. Even if I had wanted to, there was nowhere to go. I think the people saw I got cold feet. A short while passed. I exhaled. Then I heard what was like a single breath of the crowd. Like a gasp! As if the crowd had all breathed in simultaneously. It was simply incredible. I felt that gasp. I was pushed back. Maybe some two, three minutes later all the policemen were lying down. Only three or four of them, seeing what was happening, turned around and jumped the fence. They fled.

We marched on. (...) When we reached the Party Building it turned out that the doors were closed. The last of those that fled locked them shut. I looked through the window.

I saw soldiers standing motionless. Like mummies. They were armed with pistols but weren't aiming at us. There was no point in standing there. (...) No one wanted to talk to us. Later, a fight broke out there and the building was torched.

We split up into two groups. One went to Świerczewskiego St., to the Police Station, the other turned to a group of some forty policemen retreating in the direction of today's LOT building. I could see that the policemen wanted to tangle with us, but they seemed to be wavering and that's why they were retreating. I went out in front and told the policemen, "Gentlemen, there was a skirmish in front of the Shipyard a moment ago. The policemen got beat up there, so will you. Withdraw! (...) Why should we fight?

Army and police units gathering between the City HQ of the Police and Hucisko Junction. Most likely 15 December 1970.

They listened to me talk. I didn't even notice when I came into Police HQ in Świerczewskiego St. (...) I told them that we'd come for our guys who were detained there. That if they were set free then everything would end peacefully, because we didn't want to fight.

By then the crowd had reached Police HQ. The people threw rocks and the windows broke. Someone gave me a speaking tube. I stood in the window. I threw out my hardhat and time card (...) so the people could see that I too was from the Shipyard. "Stop!" I shouted. There were a lot of my mates in the crowd. I hoped they would recognise me. I managed to calm the people down for a moment. I told them that the police had agreed to let our guys go and wouldn't fight with us.

Since I didn't know those who were arrested I asked if someone would come to me and collect them. The people were happy, but it didn't last long. The entire police corps came up to the windows to look. Their commander probably didn't manage to give the order to retreat. The police downstairs attacked the Shipyard workers from two sides, trapping the crowd as if in a clamp. The crowd started calling me, "Traitor! Pig!" They thought I'd fooled them. Seconds later, thousands of rocks flew in through the windows.

*The policemen standing in the windows were taken
by surprise. They suffered casualties. Blood was shed. I was
upstairs, which is why the stones didn't reach me. I realised
that I had lost this battle. Now I had to get out of there quick.
The confusion there! Broken windows on the floor, rocks
and wounded policemen. Things were getting scary (...)*

*Slowly, slowly, I retreated from the room with the speaking
tube in my hand. They were already pulling the wounded
in when I was walking down. I found myself at the rear of
the building. I walked on. A civilian walked up to me at the
kiosk there and said, "You see? The guy failed." I broke down.*

*When I was making my way out of the HQ, a tragedy took
place. One of the policemen couldn't take the tension and
during the run-in with the crowd between the HQ and the
Presidium of the City People's Council [today's City Office
building] he took out his pistol and shot, killing a young
shipyard worker who was standing in his way. The crowd
massacred the policeman. [DN]*

December '70 in Gdańsk was the most important
event which shaped Wałęsa's political biography.
It was the first time he attempted to take events into
his own hands.

He tried to bring a rampant upheaval under control by
entering the headquarters of the police that were getting
ready for a bloody showdown. He stopped the police
commander and spoke to the crowd – played the entire
field... A self-appointed negotiator. And so it remained.
Ten years later, during the August 1980 strike, this trait
of his made people trust Wałęsa's instincts more than
any other August leader. The people felt that Wałęsa
always had another ace up his sleeve, some contingency
solution so that blood would not be shed...

Blood was shed in Gdańsk on 16 December 1970, when
unarmed shipyard workers were shot at and killed. A day

earlier, on 15 December, after the action at Police HQ, Wałęsa was elected to the Shipyard's Strike Committee.

We were afraid of a provocation. The Strike Committee and the management of the individual Departments set up night duties. (...) I stayed in Dept. W-4, with Marian Firmant on duty from the Management's side. It was calm until midnight. We took out a couple of old shipyard sheepskin coats and went to sleep. After 2 in the morning the dispatcher called, "Management with the collective are to come to the BHP Hall at 3 a.m. We took off. We were handed out copies of Głos Wybrzeża[3] daily, fresh off the presses dated already for Wednesday. Director Żaczek told us, "The Shipyard is surrounded by the military, the authorities are determined to shoot. If you want to strike, then strike, but within the Shipyard. Don't you dare leave the Shipyard. The authorities will shoot there and blood will be shed."

I thought he was just trying to scare us. (...)

The personnel came in. Everyone brought the same news, "They're everywhere: at Gates One, Two and Three. The entire Shipyard's surrounded. Tanks were lined up on both sides of the street by the Regional, Railway and Interior Ministry Hospitals. You can only get to the Shipyard through military cordons." The people reacted in different ways; most booed the soldiers. One woman shouted to them, "Sons, how can you want to shoot us?"

Something broke in the people. I don't know how to explain it, because it wasn't just their seeking revenge, but also despair and some kind of feeling of impunity. Most couldn't believe that the preparations to attack the Shipyard were true, that the authorities would dare to shoot at the workers. In our Department we did everything we could to make the people stay. Not so in other Departments. The people gathered wanted to go out into the city. It was impossible because the open gates were blocked by the military. (...)

---

[3] The official Party newspaper in the Gdańsk Coast area.

Gdańsk Shipyard Gate No. 2 in December 1970. Above it a flag at half-mast. Behind the Gate on the right is the now-gone Shipyard hospital building. In its windows hang white bed sheets with the sign of the Red Cross informing that it was a medical facility.

I was going to my Department when I heard shooting. The teeming crowd froze. From a bird-eye view it must have looked like an amoeba filling in the Shipyard streets, first one then another. It was a fury that had now frozen and shrunk. Everyone stood there petrified (...)

There were bodies lying in front of Gate No. 2. Ambulances took away the wounded; there was plenty of blood. Three guys were killed, a fourth died on the way to the hospital. They fell no more than five, maybe ten metres from the gate. A Shipyard flag was hoisted onto the mast with a black mourning ribbon. Mourning flags were also hung from the gate, together with the hardhats of the fallen with black ribbons tied around them. We commemorated the murdered with a minute of silence and sang the Polish national anthem, emphasising the words: "That which alien force has seized We at sabrepoint shall retrieve."

We installed large loudspeakers on the gates so that the duped soldiers could hear what we really wanted. The people started chanting: "Murderers, murderers!" (...) [DN]

The account of Danuta Wałęsa, Lech Wałęsa's wife

In my memory, I associate the fateful days of December '70 with our young child, our first-born son, who was a few weeks old then. On Monday, Lech bought a pram for him. On Tuesday, about noon, my husband came home for a moment (...). He was wearing his hardhat, drill work clothes and donkey jacket. He told me that terrible things were going on in Gdańsk, that blood was flowing in the streets. The next day he came home later, after four o'clock, and told me he was being followed. I remember that there was supposed to be a film on TV and that we were to go to our landlady to watch it. Just before then, two men came upstairs to take him. Lech took off his wedding band, put his watch on the table and told me that if I should be hard up, I was to sell them. And that I shouldn't worry. "It'll be alright, people will help you." On Saturday Lech's friend came and said that there would be a change in the government and that they

would surely release him. Indeed, by Sunday he was home.
He didn't say anything though – neither what they wanted
from him, nor even where they kept him, nothing. I think
he didn't want to worry me. [DN]

But being a negotiator comes with a price. This was
the first time that Wałęsa ran into the Security
Service. They located, caught and questioned
him. To this day, Wałęsa says that that very long
interrogation is the key to explain and understand
what happened. The interrogation was turned into
a document. Those in the know claim that the file
from the December interrogation still existed a dozen
or so years ago. But it has never been found.

Just like many others after December, Wałęsa was
pestered in the Shipyard. Finally, when they found
he could not be controlled, he was fired from the Shipyard
and blacklisted. But they did not cross him off their files...

Wałęsa himself does not place any importance on what
he signed then. And he got used to the constant
companionship of the secret service during various
stages of his life. He treated it as an element
of an individual game, in which he held the cards.

It can come as a shock to those who cannot believe
that one can leave a scuffle with the secret services
without losses...

December was a prelude to the entire decade that
followed it. It led to the rejection of the communist
doctrine, the break with semi-independent Poland's
Yalta-enforced dependence on the USSR, and the return
of the nation to its rightful place in Europe.

Police documentation of the march of 1 May 1971, when the marchers
carried a banner which read "We demand the punishment of those
responsible for the December incidents." Such documentation later served
to identify the march participants who demonstrated sentiments contrary
to what the communist regime wanted.

MATERIAŁ POGLĄDOWY

Egz. Nr 3

JAWNE
TAJNE

Klauzula nadana zgodnie z art. 21 Ustawy z dnia 22.01.1999 r. o ochronie informacji niejawnych

5/39

33

Materiał dowodowy

SW — 14a

34

35

36

Materiał porównawczy

Na karcie znajduje się 4 zdjęcia

In January 1971, Edward Gierek, the New First Secretary of the Central Committee of the Polish United Workers' Party met with the Gdańsk shipyard workers. On the left, Lech Wałęsa.

Towards the end of the post-December decade, Karol Cardinal Wojtyła of Cracow was chosen for the throne of the Holy See. Poland, which sought its way to freedom, had its own pope.

It was clear that a time of important breakthroughs was drawing near...

The Polish Church created a haven for people and civic activities based on moral impulse.

Opposition circles organise in Gdańsk: Komitet Obrony Robotników – KOR (Workers' Defence Committee), Ruch Obrony Praw Człowieka i Obywatela – ROPCiO (Movement for Defence of Human and Civic Rights), Wolne Związki Zawodowe Wybrzeża – WZZW (Free Trade Unions of the Coast), Ruch Młodej Polski – RMP (Young Poland Movement), and finally, Solidarity.

21/27 Okopowa St. – Presidium of the Regional People's Council (today the Pomeranian Region's Marshal's Office)

The beginning of the decade of Edward Gierek. In January 1971, a meeting held with the new First Secretary of the Party, Edward Gierek, took place here in Gdańsk, in what today is the building of the Marshal's Office, on the wave of the "normalisation" that was taking place at the time. Wałęsa was one of the three delegates from Department W-4 who went to the meeting. After the tragedy of December, there was mistrust and fear but also hope. This was the final time that Poland's communist authorities were to get the benefit of the doubt from the people. Gierek apologised for the sins of the system, promising a new style. At last, he asked, twice, urgently, "How will it be? Will you help me?" Together with the others Wałęsa replied, "We will help you!"...

The building in 21/27 Okopowa St. housed various institutions including the Regional People's Council and the magistrates' appeals court. It was here that the meeting of Edward Gierek, the First Secretary of the Party, with the Gdańsk Shipyard workers, including L. Wałęsa, took place in January 1971. This was when in reply to Gierek, the Shipyard workers shouted their famous, "We will help you!" Today, the building houses the Pomeranian Voivodeship Office and the Pomeranian Region's Marshal's Office.

Beach in the Gdańsk district of Stogi, early 1980s.

The Gdańsk district of Stogi, 26C Wrzosy St. Apt. 5, A place of their own at last...

The district lies directly by the sea on an island to the north-east of Gdańsk's historical centre. It has a beautiful, wide beach surrounded with dunes. Behind the beach is a sprawling coniferous wood with a pond. The district has a spa house. The houses are mainly villas with gardens. One can smell the mixed scents of resin and the sea in the air. This idyllic picture was shattered during the War.

For a long time after the War ended, the people of Gdańsk would argue whether the name was Stogi or maybe Sianki. The first name stuck. And just like before the War, scores of people would come here. Just as they do today. Then, as now, the tram had its last stop at a loop right by the beach. With one difference, however. It used to be that the tram, which then did not have electric closing doors, would glide along the tracks hung with "bunches" of people looking for a suntan and bathing in the sea. They would often be pursued by law enforcement officers in patrol cars, bent on fining those who would travel in such an acrobatic manner.

In the 1960s concrete blocks began to be built in Stogi for workers from the Shipyard and other factories. The blocks mixed in with the few surviving villas and allotment gardens. More and more huts were built. Even today Stogi is sociologically not unlike the Warsaw district of Praga, where not only regular, not very affluent people live, but also the so-called criminal element, which can sometimes be bothersome.

Wałęsa moved in here with his wife Danuta in 1972. Children came in rapid succession. He would commute from here to the Shipyard.

It was a working-class neighbourhood, the easternmost district from the city centre, divided from it by an industrial

area and the Motława Canal; it was a completely
different "city within a city." Our block in Wrzosy Street
neighboured huts inhabited by people similar to us, waiting
for better times. [DN]

Amber

Only a few steps away, behind the wood, was the beach.
Along it lies Gdańsk's "Klondike", areas where once
organised illegal teams of amber diggers would rinse
out amber with water pumps. There were regular battles
with the police, which would otherwise be on good terms
with the amber "bosses." [DN]

Amber has been extracted in Gdańsk for centuries.
In the Middle Ages, under the rule of the Teutonic
Order, merely gathering amber on the beach was
threatened with harsh punishment. In time, amber
artefacts became one of Gdańsk's most recognisable
trademarks in Europe. It is enough to recall the famous
Amber Room, designed by 18th century Gdańsk
craftsmen, and whose fate captured the imaginations
of treasure hunters for decades.

This amber El Dorado boomed anew with new found
force during the construction of the Northern Port,
founded here as part of Gierek's big investment plan
which also included the construction of an oil refinery.
People would whisper that the piers, first the Coal
Pier, then the Fuel Pier, were to cut off our dependence
on our eastern neighbour, giving Poland the status
of an independent exporter and importer...

This was when the amber fortunes were born.
The illegal extraction of hundreds of kilograms
of the Gold of the Baltic would be sold by the diggers
from Stogi (also illegally) to Gdańsk amber jewellers.

Stogi, building in 26 Wrzosy St. where Danuta and Lech Wałęsa moved in 1972. They lived here until the first days of September 1980. The concrete blocks for the workers of the Shipyard and other workplaces began to be built in the 1960s.

They would in turn craft the amber into rings, necklaces and other gems which they would sell to tourists in the city or export, usually by smuggling, to the West. Some of these fortunes, however, disappeared overnight. They were flushed away with the glasses of vodka and whisky and the nightly thrills at the infamous Relax bar in Stogi.

Today, prospectors can lease amber-bearing land from the city and amber can be extracted legally.

Today, the Foregate Complex with its austere Torture House and Prison Tower in Gdańsk's historic Main Town houses Poland's only Amber Museum, which exhibits unique specimens of the Gold of the Baltic with Gierłowska's Lizard trapped in a resinous nugget as one of its highlights. Every year Gdańsk hosts the Amberif Fair, the world's only trade exhibition dedicated to amber, which attracts jewellers and traders from Europe, America and Asia. And so Gdańsk has certainly earned its moniker as the World Capital of Amber.

Lech Wałęsa and family in the late 1970s. Gdańsk 'Milk Can' Towers in the background.

Children are born

We had our small flat in Wrzosy St. and Danuta and I remember those years as a period when we grew close forever. Those were happy times for us as a family, even though we lived very modestly. (...)

We moved in to Stogi as a foursome: with two sons, Bogdan and Sławek, who was two months old then. Our next children were born in fairly regular intervals so we associated almost every birth with an extraordinary event and we often reminisce according to this family calendar.

With Bogdan it was December '70, Sławek – our moving to Stogi, Przemek – my getting fired from the Shipyard, Jarek – my first contacts with the Free Trade Unions, Magda, when she was still in her pram got to be the youngest person to be arrested together with me when we were taken to Police HQ, Ania came along during the strike and Solidarity, Maria Wiktoria was born when I was interned; I saw her for the first time when she was several months old and Danuta brought her to Arłamów, and finally Brygida, the youngest. (...)

Danuta and Lech Wałęsa with sons on the beach.

We were young and happy with our family. We often took all five of our children for walks through the wood in Stogi to the beach, where I would swim in the summertime after work, or in the opposite direction: to the Old Town, to the River Motława, to visit Danuta's aunt in Heweliusza St. and to the monument in Westerplatte. The biggest problem was in the evening, when we had to wash and feed all five of them and put them to bed. We had to unfold the beds every night and when the kids got bigger, the mattresses and beds took up almost the entire flat, meaning two small rooms, one of which was a one-and-a-half metre narrow "squeeze-belly" room, while the other served as a living room with a divan bed, a small children's bed and a table. The sewing machine in the corner sometimes served as a pedestal for a primitive press where we would print leaflets. [DN]

View of buildings in former Kalinowskiego St. (now Targ Rakowy), including the Regional Trade Union Council. (Today the building houses the Regional and City Public Library.) In the foreground, the unveiling of the monument to Maria Konopnicka, November 1977.

Kalinowskiego St. (today the Lobster Market), WRZZ (the trade union sanctioned by the communist regime) headquarters; the Security Service controls the Shipyard; there is tapping everywhere and summons are given "for talks"

Six years after the meeting with Gierek, Wałęsa was mad at himself for saying "We will help you." This forced reply was constantly shown on television as proof of the working class's support for the First Secretary of the Party. In his rebellious addresses at union meetings at the Shipyard, Wałęsa called the official union a "dummy union" and criticised the propaganda-based launching of vessels ahead of schedule, as they later would have to be equipped and finished. He would criticise Gierek for breaking his promises. He was a target for the Security Service, which was causing him problems since his first arrest in December 1970.

Formally speaking, I was still a Department delegate to the company trade union with the right to vote. I was called up to the Management, where the Security Service was already waiting for me.

"Sir," they said, "do not deliver that speech. Say you're a delegate. Will you say what we will prepare for you, or do you want to do it your way?"

"Oh no, gentlemen, I'll do it my way. Even if you give me a slip of paper, I'll switch it at the last moment."

"Then fall ill or go on a holiday. You can't go to the conference!"

"No, gentlemen, I'll go even with a fever."

So they got on the phone, then the guards grabbed me by the arms and led me out the gate, and that was the end of it.
[DN]

When he was fired from the Shipyard on 30 April 1976,
Wałęsa went to the Regional Trade Union Council
(Wojewódzka Rada Związków Zawodowych – WRZZ)
in Kalinowskiego St. Today the building houses
the Regional and City Public Library. Wałęsa filed
a complaint but to no avail: WRZZ was at the Security
Service's bidding. If anyone had any illusions about the
agenda of this phoney institution, it was enough to look
upon the Soviet tank-monument standing in front
of the building: where Soviet tanks reached in 1945,
the order and system decreed by Stalin in Yalta ruled.
The communist authorities in Poland acted according
to this plan, with the Security Service methodically
doing the dirty work. This was a far cry from the hope
unfolded for the country by Edward Gierek...

30/ 40 Siennicka St., the ZREMB Construction Machine Factory

Siennicka St. leads from the centre of Gdańsk to
the Przeróbka district then further on to Stogi. Here,
in the fork of the Rivers Motława and Martwa Wisła,
there were various industrial plants, including a meat-
packing plant, the Calypso ice cream factory, companies
working for the maritime economy and a big scrapyard.

As we can read in an extant factory chronicle:

*The war left terrible destruction throughout the country.
In this difficult time, when there was a shortage of specialists
and equipment to rebuild the destroyed houses and factories,
the consciousness of creating a new tomorrow dawned.
And so, in August 1945, the Central Material
Agency in Warsaw (...) ordered our factory to organise
the construction materials and equipment coming from
UNRRA[4] deliveries and army surplus.*

---

[4] The United Nations Relief and Rehabilitation Administration.

Thanks to the waterway and the railway siding, the location was perfect. And so "Aunt UNRRA", as it was called back then, sent diggers and bulldozers. They were repaired here and sent on.

Today, the old meat-packing plant in Angielska Grobla St., which used to be a nuisance to the locals for decades because of its smell, is no more. Also gone is the transport department of the ZREMB Construction Machine Factory in Gdańsk, where Lech Wałęsa found work in May 1976 when he was dismissed from the Shipyard and where he worked until 31 January 1979. Storehouses, wholesale stores and various larger and smaller companies now stand in its place. There is a grocery store in the small porter's house at the former entrance gate. ZREMB itself is still in business in the Orunia district in Trakt Świętego Wojciecha St. (formerly Jedności Robotniczej St.). It no longer employs several hundred people like it did in the 1970s; its employment is ten times less today.

We ran into financial problems when they threw me out of the Shipyard, so I immediately went to work in the nearby ZREMB Construction Machine Repair plant. They employed me in the car repair department and I liked the job. As one of the few electricians in the car department I was often sent for by the management in Orunia, where I got to know a couple of new people. After two months of observation which continued from my time at the Shipyard, the Security Service finally got off my back, watching me from afar, and stopped bothering me. I started to put together a car for myself out of old parts. Nearby ZREMB there was a scrapyard, where they would put old run-down Warszawa cars which were taken off the roads. I bought one such car for four and a half thousand zlotys and repaired it. We took that old Warszawa on a holiday to Danuta's home area. My salary improved and I did odd jobs on the side, repairing peoples' cars. One would recommend me to another and so I always had something to do. [DN]

The Free Trade Unions of the Coast (WZZW)

I was an easy target, because I was well known for my activism at the Shipyard. After December, the papers Głos Wybrzeża and Wieczór Wybrzeża, wrote about me as a person who "got his experience during the strike" and "expresses the interests of the working class." They tried to flatter me. (...) [DN]

There was the temptation of an easy life.

But Lech Wałęsa was looking for a group to form that he could join.

I first heard about the Free Trade Unions of the Coast and the Young Poland Movement when I laid wreaths at the gate of the Shipyard on 1 May 1978. (...)

I got hold of an issue of The Coastal Worker (Robotnik Wybrzeża), probably through Bogdan Borusewicz, who I had met at the time. It so happened that the issue included a declaration of the establishment of the Free Trade Unions of the Coast (WZZW), complete with an address and a name. (...) They weren't doing very well as they operated in a small isolated group, not many people knew about them and the participation of workers in their operation was practically zero. I went to Wyszkowski's home where I met Andrzej and Joanna Gwiazda and I told them that they had to do it another way. The founders of the WZZ were targeted by the authorities: I think Błażej Wyszkowski was arrested, Antoni Sokołowski had a breakdown and the newly formed group came close to disbanding. I decided that, no matter what happened, I had to join them and prevent the organisation from falling apart. Later, Anna Walentynowicz joined and everything began to work better. [DN]

For KOR, WZZ, RMP and ROPCiO activists
– a circle made up almost exclusively from
intellectuals – Wałęsa, as one of the few "real workers,"
was a somewhat exotic phenomenon:

Bogdan Lis

*I met him in 1978 ... It was the anniversary of the events
of December 1970 at Andrzej Gwiazda's home. I remember
how Wałęsa spoke about the sequence of events which he took
part in.* [FD]

Bogdan Borusewicz

*(...) He was out of work, but began to organise in Stogi,
which was a very, very difficult area, one could well call
it a "lumpenproletariat" area.* [FD]

Bożena Rybicka-Grzywaczewska

*Together with Magda Modzelewska we ran a prayer
service in St Mary's Church. One time a gentleman
in a blue uniform-like suit showed up with a group of much
younger boys.* [FD]

Bogdan Borusewicz

There was one thing that made him stand out: the whiskers.
[FD]

Bożena Rybicka-Grzywaczewska

*He always carried around a bunch of leaflets with him
so he could barely button up his jacket.* [FD]

Bogdan Borusewicz

*It turned out that he had his own car, a sort of Nysa van,
which he put together on a Warszawa chassis. When you saw
that Nysa, you could immediately tell you were dealing with
someone interesting. First of all, he had a car; all of us lived*

quite modestly, we didn't even have our own flats, because we were young people active in the opposition, we couldn't even dream of having a car. And then here comes a guy who says, "I've got a car and you can use it."

He had really poor living conditions; he had two rooms and five children. At the time, when we would come to him to talk, we would have to lock up the kids in the bathroom. [FD]

Bogdan Lis

He had the courage to take certain decisions, to take risks, because then, in 1970, there was no one to defend the people who would later come to Borusewicz, who fell foul of the authorities. [FD]

Bogdan Borusewicz

In the second half of 1977, our strength was our camaraderie, one could even say, the affection we had for each other. Every one of us knew that we would go through fire and water for each other. [FD]

Lech Kaczyński

We certainly were a significant group and it's actually strange that this group fell out with each other as much as it did. I wouldn't blame Lech Wałęsa so much for it. The situation was quite tense already at the time of the Free Trade Unions, which was normal insofar as, although Lech Wałęsa was a very important member of the Free Trade Unions, he wasn't the most important, whereas later he became the most important not only in the Free Trade Unions, not only in Solidarity, but in Poland in general. [FD]

ZREMB – meeting of the Workers' Self-Management Conference

In the autumn of 1978, Wałęsa protested against the Party's pushing of candidates to trade union authorities:

I got up then and said, "Gentlemen, what am I here for, if everything has already been decided? Something's wrong here; I've got this brochure by Jacek Kuroń where he writes that what you're doing is nonsense."

(...) I stuck it to them and some time after the meeting I got dismissed from work. They laid me off. One car electrician post and they get rid of it. Obviously I knew why, but they wouldn't write why, of course, "factory reorganisation, the post is unnecessary." Even though I was my family's sole provider. [DN]

Hourglass made by the opposition, which informed the people of Gdańsk about the December ceremonies by the Gdańsk Shipyard in 1979.

The wall of Gdańsk Shipyard next to Gate No. 2; in 1978 and 1979 the site of illegal demonstrations commemorating the anniversaries of December 1970

(...) I also had participation in the commemoration of the eighth anniversary of December 1970 on my record. We decided to commemorate it in a solemn way. On the day when everything was ready, the wreaths were bought, the group was organised, there was a raid. They even arrested people going to the cemeteries with flowers. The police carried out a broad series of house searches and our entire group was arrested. It turned out that I got special treatment: my colleagues were released after a few hours, in the afternoon when the best time for a public demonstration had passed, while I remained in prison for two days. We didn't give up; when I got out, we met again three days later. We got to the Shipyard wall at about 2 p.m. and fell right into the hands of the police. They were waiting for us the whole time. And so we were arrested again. This time Borusewicz remained in prison for two days, while I was tried in a magistrates' court as a "hooligan," who disturbed the public peace. Five days later I was dismissed from work. I was now unemployed. But by now we were a group. Over the last few weeks of 1978, the police carried out some 70 house searches and made some 140 arrests throughout the Tri-City. That meant that there were a lot of us. [DN]

In the late 1970s, the Gdańsk democratic opposition organised demonstrations commemorating the tragic events of December 1970 by the Gdańsk Shipyard. The authorities would try anything to prevent them. The photograph shows buses parked along the Shipyard wall, which were to prevent the gathering of demonstrators and the laying of wreaths.

Elektromontaż Plant, 7 Wosia Budzysza St. – Wałęsa escapes from the Security Service hidden in a container

On the boundary between Przeróbka and Stogi, in Wosia Budzysza St., is the transport and equipment base of the Elektromontaż Electric Construction Equipment Manufacturing Plant (Woś Budzysz was the pen name of Kashubian writer and activist Jan Karnowski). Wałęsa was hired as a vehicle electrician here in early May 1979. In contrast to ZREMB this former workplace of Wałęsa is still there.

Elektromontaż was the site of some of his best and most memorable operations. He distributed the *Robotnik, The War of Independence with Russia 1918–1920* and *Katyń* any way he could and as much as he could. He formed the Workers' Committee. He brought a tape recorder with a recording of a show from Radio Free Europe about the opposition in Poland and played it to his colleagues. For this he was fired in early February 1980.

The most famous, however, remains his escape in the container.

The next, ninth anniversary of December was drawing near. They arrested everyone starting with Borusewicz, who was already in jail for two weeks. I was practically alone, except for the youngsters from the Young Poland Movement. They were out to get me. I wouldn't come home for the night, because the Security Service was waiting for me in Stogi. I still managed to get to work because the people knew what was going on and helped me. The Security Service surrounded the entire factory and searched for me in the halls (...) and throughout the premises until my colleagues put me in a container, sealed it up and so I managed to get out of Elektromontaż in spite of the raid. I got to Gate No. 2 at the Shipyard in time; the youngsters Dariusz Kobzdej and Maryla Płońska were just finishing their speeches.

I spoke of December 1970 and concluded by urging everyone to join together to build a monument to the fallen Shipyard workers next year: everyone was to bring a handful of stones, and drop them on a pile in order to form a mound like the Kościuszko Mound in Cracow. [DN]

Piwna St. across from St Mary's Church, police station and prison

Next door was the job centre and the magistrates' court.

After each firing Wałęsa would come here to look for work. Just as often he would be sent to prison for his activity in the opposition.

I broke the unwritten rule that a prisoner was supposed to be ashamed. That's what the authorities who tried to crush us with police methods wanted. When I would come from my arrests in the morning, usually with my pockets raked and without a penny, I liked to tell the other passengers on the tram what had happened. I would tell them that I spent two days in prison just because I wanted to commemorate my Shipyard colleagues who died in December, that I took part in the celebration of banned patriotic anniversaries. The people, though surprised at first, reacted in a lively and usually friendly way, giving me a ticket home; they would take up the conversation and ask for details... [DN]

Jacek Taylor, lawyer

Wałęsa was tried at the Magistrates' Court for an attempt to lay a wreath at the Shipyard in 1978, in the place where the Monument now stands. (...) On top of that, the December anniversaries always ended up with Lech being imprisoned for two days, after which they would summarily put him before the magistrates' court. The court would sentence him to the maximum fine: 5 thousand zlotys, plus 150 zlotys administrative fees.

*I was with Wałęsa at the magistrates' appeals court.
The trials would take place on Holy Saturday, Easter Eve.
The idea was to have no public present. Both trials were
in Okopowa St., and there were only Security Service officers
present in the courtroom. (...)*

*In the early 1980s, he again stood before the magistrates.
This time for" (...) driving a Warszawa passenger car
without the required lighting in conditions of insufficient
visibility. The summoned drove said vehicle which was
technically defective (no right headlight or stop light, faulty
auxiliary brake), which was a threat to traffic safety."* [RJT]

The real reason for seizing the car was a sticker
about the December anniversary on the windscreen.
Even though the witnesses, policemen, got their
testimonies mixed up and the evidence was
questionable, the magistrates sentenced Wałęsa
to a fine of 3 thousand zlotys and fees of 100 zlotys.
What is worse, they also took away his driver's licence
for a year. Right after August, the authorities quietly
gave Wałęsa his licence back.

Wałęsa not only appeared before the courts in his
own cases, but also came to the trials of other
dissident as a show of solidarity. He acted according
to his worker's ethos.

Arkadiusz Rybicki

*It was when Błażej Wyszkowski was tried before
the magistrates. He was a WZZ trade union activist, but
an intellectual. The courtroom was full of Security Service
officers; "there weren't enough tickets" for the opposition
people. We were waiting in the corridor. Then Wałęsa came
up with two workers at his side and said, "Well then?
We got a trial, so we'll do them in..."* [PZM]

Stogi, Wrzosy St. – Wałęsa organises a leaflet printing group

Danuta Wałęsa

Until 1980 I knew about his involvement with the Free Trade Unions, but I wasn't privy to many details. I once went to a Free Trade Unions meeting. Once there was a funeral of one of the activists and the Security Service came for my husband. They put him, the wreath and his colleagues in the car. I began to shout and beat my shoe on the car. And so the neighbours in our block of flats got to know about the Free Trade Unions, that the Security Service was watching us and that something was going on. My husband wouldn't disclose much to me, always saying that he didn't want me to be affected. The idea was that since I didn't know where he was going I wouldn't worry that he might get arrested or – God forbid! – get killed. I did the same to protect our children. I didn't tell them many things so that they wouldn't worry that something might happen to their mother and father. [DW]

The spring of 1980, which preceded the August strike at the Gdańsk Shipyard, saw the height of Wałęsa's dissident activities. He was imprisoned and tried before the magistrates' court. He was everywhere: at WZZW trade union training courses run by Doctor Lech Kaczyński, in the Morena district, at home in Stogi... He ran a sort of underground cell with his neighbours and boldly distributed dozens of thousands of leaflets in the Old Town of Gdańsk.

Józef Drogoń, worker

The only thing that the people in Stogi knew about Lech was that he was guy who was a bit of a gadfly, got arrested by the police, that he was fighting for something, demanding something, but no one really knew exactly what it was. (...)

*I lived in Stogi very near to Lech. Lech thought that
everyone who wanted to could come to him. When the
time came to spread leaflets, like on 3 May[5], after Kobzdej
and Szczudłowski were arrested, anyone who wanted to
could join us. Lech activated Stogi, which was a dodgy
neighbourhood where the people minded their own business.
For them Wałęsa was just a neighbour and that was it.
He took two or three of us, we took a pack of leaflets and
took them round the apartment blocks in Stogi. For instance
me and Ewa Ossowska, a newsagent, who stood on guard
at one of the gates in the Shipyard in August, dark-haired;
I went with her once (...) Lech would sometimes surprise me.
One day he said, "Eat lunch and come over." So I came over
and sat down. Lech had a typewriter and paper. That was
in April, maybe May 1980. He wanted me to roll out
the Union Movement (Ruch Związkowy) newsletter.
It was just a regular roller and a pane, someone put it
together for him.* [DN]

Football traditions

There was one more interesting event that happened
in Stogi. Just before August, a famous football
match between the WZZW (Free Trade Unions
of the Coast) and the RMP (Young Poland Movement)
took place there.

*It was a rather uneven pitch. The important thing was that
there were two goalposts there. We had a lot of problems
at the start of the match, because there was a horse grazing
on the field and it couldn't care less about our passion for
football. We were all afraid to approach the horse to take
it to another place. We were all looking at each other.
Then Lech came on the scene. He calmly approached the horse,
patted it, took the reins and led it off the pitch.* [SR]

---

[5] Constitution Day, banned by the communist authorities.

As usual, Aleksander Hall was the RMP goalie;
Lech Wałęsa stood between the posts for WZZW.
Everyone wondered why there were no secret
policemen, who always hung around when a large
group of dissidents gathered. When towards the end
of the match RMP was leading 4 : 3 and it seemed
that Young Poland would win, one of them handled
the ball. A penalty kick led to a goal and the match
ended in a draw. Several weeks later, after August,
it turned out that the guy who had handled the ball was
a Security Service collaborator. They didn't need to have
any secret policemen at the match. They had a mole...

There were no dissident salons at Gdańsk like they had
in Warsaw or literary and actors' circles like in Warsaw
and Cracow – meeting places for the unofficial elite.
Here the opposition was formed by young people who
liked to play football and were supporters of Lechia
Gdańsk. That is why football matches became a peculiar
Gdańsk phenomenon. The football match tradition
that began before August survived the difficult 1980s.
In fact, it got stronger. We have had historic matches
between the dissidents working in the Gdańsk Świetlik
Co-op, the "holy wars" between the Young Poland
activists and the editors of the underground *Przegląd
Polityczny* (Political Review), where Donald Tusk came
from. In time, the football playing came to the capital.
The current prime minister plays, so do MPs,
Jan Krzysztof Bielecki, the former prime minister,
now the CEO of Pekao SA, one of the largest banks
in Poland, all of them came from here...

Lech Wałęsa at the match between Lechia Gdańsk and Juventus Turin in the Cup Winners' Cup. At halftime almost 40 thousand spectators rallied to show their support for the underground Solidarity and Wałęsa. 28 September 1983.

Lechia Gdańsk Stadium, 29 Traugutta St.

When we reminisce about the former dissidents' hobby of football, we cannot fail to mention the political attitude of Lechia Gdańsk supporters. On Poland's football map appeared a place where the communist reality was regularly and openly negated. That place was the stadium of the white and greens: the colours of Lechia Gdańsk.

It started right after the tragic December '70.
In the spring of 1971, Lechia played an important away game in Poznań and over a thousand supporters from Gdańsk travelled to see it. As Mirosław Rybicki, football player and future activist of the Young Poland Movement, recalls:

The sectors taken up by Lechia supporters were tightly surrounded by armed police forces. The atmosphere was very tense. The police staged an anti-Gdańsk demonstration of force. The idea was not to watch over unruly supporters, but to intimidate the people of Gdańsk. Our answer was to chant, "We'll repeat December!" [BZS]

From the time when martial law was enacted, up until 1989, there wasn't a match that went by without the fanatical Lechia supporters expressing their support for the underground Solidarity. Anti-communist slogans were regularly chanted and Solidarity banners were regularly hung.

One of the most important days in the club's, but not only the club's, history was 28 September 1983. Juventus Turin came to Gdańsk. The famous Italian club, with its many stars led by Zbigniew Boniek and Michel Platini (now the president of UEFA) played a match in the Cup Winners' Cup with a Cinderella team.

*That was a difficult time for Solidarity and for Wałęsa
personally. The Security Service fabricated a recording
of Wałęsa and his brother, trying to convince his countrymen
that Lech was up to some shady business. These fabricated
recordings were played on TV. We had to do everything
to have Lech show himself at this important match. I got my
friends together, who sat right after the stadium gates opened
directly across from the grandstand, where all the Party
and Security Service bigwigs were seated. When we passed
the police cordons without incident – strangely enough,
Lech wasn't recognised – we sat with Wałęsa at the agreed
place just before the opening whistle. A big commotion
ensued at half-time. We started chanting "Solidarity"
and "Lech Wałęsa" and so everyone quickly knew that
Wałęsa was at the stadium. [SR]*

*The incredible demonstration lasted for more than a dozen
minutes. Over 30 thousand people chanting: "Lech Wałęsa,"
"Solidarity" and "We will win!" The state television refused
to resume live coverage before the show of support ended.*

*The authorities didn't give in, however. The next day
the Głos Wybrzeża Party newspaper published an article
referring to the fabricated recording on TV. Part of the article
was purposefully put in the sports section next to the match
recap. Of course there was nothing about the pro-Wałęsa
and pro-Solidarity demonstration. [BZS]*

But let's now return to the streets of Gdańsk,
the time is the sunny summer of 1980...

St Dominic's Fair, the historical centre of Gdańsk, Długa, Długie Pobrzeże, Świętego Ducha and Mariacka St.s

Józef Drogoń

Lech, Sylwek Niezgoda and the entire group would scatter leaflets in Długa St. during St Dominic's Fair. They would scatter the leaflets by hand. Everyone had four packs fixed behind their belts. You would throw them up in the air with your hand and they would scatter; we would take advantage of the breeze coming from the Green Gate so that the wind would carry the leaflets all the way up to the roofs. It was after lunch, after work, there were a lot of people there, so there were many who could pick them up.

The guys would walk from four sides from St Mary's Church, depending on which direction the wind was blowing. The one who was doing the throwing was covered by two others who protected him from the police. They would stage a scuffle so that the thrower could quickly run away. The operation was a success. Lech was there, he took part in all those operations. [DN]

Chmielna and Piwna St. – The police station Magda Wałęsa is arrested

That was the second time I was arrested with Lech. We scattered leaflets in the old market in Chmielna St. (...) Lech did the throwing and I watched over his few-month-old daughter Magda in her pram. When Lech saw he was being targeted, he took the pram from me and we went in the direction of Elbląska St. There were beer gardens there with umbrellas by the Gdańsk Sailing Co. They arrested us there: myself, Lech and the kid. (...)

Lech pushed the pram, the policemen followed him, I was taken in a van. At the police station the kid peed on the floor and the officer on duty, a sergeant, said, "Wipe that up now!" Lech replied, "You wipe it up. You locked up the child, you change her nappy, I'm not going to do it." She cried because it was cold, even though it was July; she sensed something was wrong. [DN]

The Gdańsk dissidents printed several dozen thousand leaflets in defence of the imprisoned Dariusz Kobzdej and Tadeusz Szczudłowski. Some say that as many as one hundred thousand may have been printed. In any event, there was revolution in the air in Gdańsk in the early summer of 1980.

St Mary's Church

This monumental church standing in the very heart of historical Gdańsk is a symbolic place not only because of its size. It was here that in the latter half of the 1970s Father Józef Zator-Przytocki, lieutenant-colonel of the Home Army[6], recipient of the Order of Virtuti Militari, began celebrating masses for the homeland organised by the Young Poland Movement to celebrate 11 November (Independence Day) and 3 May (Constitution Day), banned by the Polish Peoples' Republic. It was immediately after such a mass that on 11 November 1978 the first patriotic demonstration of the Gdańsk opposition went to the monument of King John III Sobieski.

In a side chapel, before the image of Our Lady of the Gate of Dawn, regular public prayers were said aloud in 1980 for the release of those arrested after the demonstration on 3 May. Lech Wałęsa took part in these services.

View of St Mary's Church. The people of Gdańsk built this church for 159 years; it is the largest brick church in the world. Its total capacity is ca. 155,000 cubic metres, length: 105.5 m, width in the transept: 66 m. The largest window has an area of 127 square metres. The bell tower is 82 m high (up to the ridge). The church has a capacity of ca. 20 thousand. Its visitors have included Polish kings, Swedish kings, Tsar Peter the Great, Napoleon Bonaparte and many contemporary VIPs. Badly damaged in March 1945. In the late 1970s Gdańsk democratic opposition activists organised patriotic masses here on national holidays on 3 May and 11 November, which were banned by the regime.

---

[6] The chief Polish underground military organisation during World War II.

A decade of the rosary was prayed with the intention: "Mother of God, we commend to your care our friends: Dariusz Kobzdej, Tadeusz Szczudłowski, Bogdan Grzesiak. We join with them in prayer, especially now when they are awaiting their retrials. Please keep them in good health and that they persevere in the hope of the power of truth and justice." Wałęsa was among those who read out the intentions. [PZM]

The rectory of St Mary's parish in 5 Podkramarska St. would later play another role. In the 1980s it was the place of regular meetings between Wałęsa and advisors to the outlawed Solidarity. Archbishop Tadeusz Gocłowski recalls:

In 1982, Archbishop Bronisław Dąbrowski, the secretary of the Episcopate, decided that we should take care of Lech Wałęsa during the difficult martial law period. I played the role of political chaperone. The Episcopate decided that the advisers to Solidarity, who lived in Warsaw, should be able to come to Gdańsk and meet with Mr Wałęsa on church premises. I was asked to accompany Wałęsa as a bishop so that the authorities would not harass him. We would meet in the home of Father Stanisław Bogdanowicz. We would eat lunch in the rectory, and after that would be an hour or an hour-and-a-half long conversation. Every month, Messrs Mazowiecki, Wielowieyski, Bugaj, Geremek and others would come: the Solidarity advisers. We suspected we were bugged so we would change the places where we held the conversation. Sometimes they would take place in the dining room on the ground floor, other times we would go upstairs. [TG]

The greeting of Dariusz Kobzdej (with flowers) upon his release from jail in front of the entrance to St Mary's Church on 6 August 1980. Kobzdej and Tadeusz Szczudłowski were sentenced to three months in prison for delivering speeches at a patriotic demonstration to commemorate the national holiday of the May 3 Constitution in front of the monument to King John III Sobieski. In the chapel of Our Lady of the Gate of Dawn, prayers were said for the release of political prisoners. The prayers were led by Bożena Rybicka (to Kobzdej's left) and Magdalena Modzelewska together with Lech Wałęsa.

Wrzeszcz, 10 Henryka Sienkiewicza St. Apt. 6, home of Piotr Dyk. It was here that the decision to take strike action took place on 14 August 1980

The strike of 1980 was a masterpiece. It was the sum of the experience of the Polish people and of Wałęsa himself. The management, under pressure from the Security Service, fired Anna Walentynowicz, who was well known and respected, five months before retirement. The Gdańsk opposition groups did their homework – they printed and distributed illegal newsletters and leaflets; the awareness about Polish history was growing – uprisings, partitions, the Constitution of the 3rd of May, the Katyń massacre, the lack of independence and the political and economic dependence on the USSR. The "cinema of moral concern" trend arrived, including Andrzej Wajda's clearly rebellious Man of Marble. And then there was the Polish pope in the Vatican.

During the twenty-fifth anniversary of August '80, Wałęsa looked back...

Lech Wałęsa at the Roads to Freedom Exhibition

We fought for values. We fought for the whole world; for Germany to unite... And that was the whole secret. When the whole world lacked a vision of how to change the world, how to end communism, Poland got a boon with the Pope. At the time I had ten people organised, out of a nation of forty million, and if not for the Holy Father it would have taken me another twenty years to organise the next ten. And then the Pope came to Poland, and spoke the famous words, "Do not be afraid, change the face of the Earth." A year after he left, we were able to organise ten million people ready to change the world. [FD]

Before the strike

The strike in the Lenin Shipyard in Gdańsk was organised by Bogdan Borusewicz. He had three young workers at the Shipyard to help him: Jerzy Borowczak, Ludwik Prądzyński and Bogdan Felski. They were to get the Shipyard going. But the wildcard in the strike was to be Lech Wałęsa, currently unemployed, a man with experience from the strike of 1970, a husband and father, and finally, a former Shipyard worker, who the crew knew.

The day was Sunday, 10 August 1980.
In the apartment of Piotr Dyk of the Young Poland Movement in 10 Sienkiewicza St. in the Gdańsk district of Wrzeszcz, the Gdańsk opposition greeted Dariusz Kobzdej and Tadeusz Szczudłowski, who had been released after three months in jail. Some did more than just greet...

Bogdan Borusewicz

Wałęsa found out about the date of the strike a couple of days before; it was on Saturday or Sunday. Sunday, I think. In Wrzeszcz, Sienkiewicza St. A great big apartment; the only big apartment at the opposition's disposal. A lot of people came and I called Felski, Borowczak, Prądzyński and Lech out into the courtyard, because the apartment was obviously bugged. Then I told them that we would do the strike on Thursday. The arrangements were brief, because all one could arrange was how it would start; we knew we would have to improvise from then on. The boys said, "Just you come, Lech, we're scared, we've got to have someone older." And come he did, although somewhat later – they bore a grudge against him for that, but he made it, the important thing was that he made it. If you ask, "Was he the one who was ready to be the leader?" Everyone was ready to be the leader... theoretically. [FD]

Tram No. 8 from Stogi to the strike, 14 August 1980

At daybreak leaflets appeared in the trams and
the railway trains. Their main topic was the case
of Anna Walentynowicz, dismissed from the Shipyard
on disciplinary grounds a week before.

There are a number of detailed reports on how that
day began for Wałęsa. There is a report by a Security
Service officer who followed Wałęsa on 14 August
– from the door of his block of flats in Wrzosy St.
to the Shipyard wall at Rybaki Górne St.

In his biography Wałęsa tells about the day:

*I got to the strike by tram. Alone. In decisive moments
you're usually alone. I had a bit of time. Different thoughts
went through my head. Why weren't they arresting me?
I saw characteristic civilians around me. They were right
next to me, any reason would do. The Shipyard had been
on strike since six in the morning, so by now, about eight,
they knew everything.*

*I heard the sirens while still at home; I knew it had begun.
I couldn't leave earlier, I had to get my house in order. (...)*

*I got in the tram. The ride was long, it took a good thirty-
five minutes to get from Stogi to the Shipyard. I became
increasingly suspicious over this time. They had me covered
tight; I saw them in their car, they guarded me well. So it
must have suited them somehow? What were they planning?
Were they counting on change at our expense, from which
they would profit? What could it be? Or maybe they were
waiting for us to show our hand and then they would strike
us all at once? (...)*

*There was already a commotion at Gate No. 2, but the
guards carefully checked the security passes and I hadn't
been allowed into the Shipyard in years. I turned right,
in the direction of Gate No. 1, and there, between the gates,*

by the school, where there is a small side-street; I walked there and jumped over the wall. [DN]

Meanwhile, at the Shipyard, events were rapidly developing according to the scenario sketched by Bogdan Borusewicz; an improvised rally was held in front of the management building.

Bogdan Felski

(...) (The) Director (of the Shipyard) Gniech, appeared. He took the floor. He wanted us to get back to work. He promised negotiations. The Director also spoke to the crowd from an excavator. Then Leszek Wałęsa appeared from nowhere behind the Director.

"Do you recognise me, sir? Ten years ago I worked in the Shipyard and I still consider myself a Shipyard worker, since I have the trust of the crew. I've been unemployed for four years now!", Wałęsa said this very loudly. The situation was a bit comical. "We're starting a sit-in strike!" shouted Wałęsa to the crowd. "Hooray!" rang out from the entire Shipyard. Then we demanded that Ms Walentynowicz be brought to the Shipyard in the Director's car. The Director protested, but his car went for Ms Anna. We rushed to the Shipyard radio broadcasting system. That's how the strike began. [DN]

This address will forever remain etched in Polish history:

Gdańsk Shipyard with its Gate No. 2 and the famous BHP Hall, where the delegates from the strikers of the Tri-City and the entire country assembled: shown in all the world's media as a place where the self-restraining, self-controlled Solidarity revolution, fulfilling the appeal of the Polish Pope, indeed changed the face of the Earth.

On 31 August 1980 Wałęsa said his famous words:

(...) we got everything that we could get in the current situation. We'll get the rest too, because we've got the most important thing: our own independent, self-governing trade unions. This is our guarantee for the future! [ZRG]

This is how the Solidarity Independent Self-Governing Trade Union was born – the first legal organisation independent of the authorities in the entire communist bloc. Just a trade union? No, it was something far more important: a great, almost ten million strong civic movement for freedom. A beacon of hope not only for Poles and Poland.

The signing of the Gdańsk Agreement at the BHP Hall between the Inter-Factory Strike Committee in the Lenin Shipyard in Gdańsk and the Government Commission. To the left of L. Wałęsa is Deputy Prime Minister Mieczysław Jagielski, on the right: Inter-Factory Strike Committee Presidium member Florian Wiśniewski, Gdańsk Voivode Jerzy Kołodziejski, Inter-Factory Strike Committee presidium members Wojciech Gruszecki and Henryka Krzywonos.

As the British historian Timothy Garton Ash noted:

(...) no other movement in the world was supported simultaneously by President Reagan, eurocommunists Carrillo and Berlinguer and the pope, by Margaret Thatcher, peace activists and NATO spokespeople, Christians and communists, conservatives, liberals and socialists. [TGA]

Years later, in 2003, UNESCO entered the Gdańsk plywood boards with the twenty-one demands made by the Inter-Factory Strike Committee in Gdańsk Shipyard in its World Heritage List. The same boards that hung by the Shipyard's Gate No. 2.

Lech Wałęsa speaking to the crowds gathered in front of Gdańsk Shipyard's Gate No. 2 on 31 August 1980, directly after the signing of the Gdańsk Agreement, which provided for, among other things, the establishment of Independent Self-Governing Trade Unions. In his right hand he holds the famous pen with the picture of John Paul II, with which he signed the agreement with the Polish Peoples' Republic government delegation.

Gdańsk-Wrzeszcz, 13 Marchlewskiego St. (now Dmowskiego St.) – Solidarity's first headquarters

Then, on 31 August 1980, the history of Gdańsk and Poland entered a new chapter, as did the biography of the strike's leader.

The place of the headquarters of the new trade union was settled even before the Agreement was signed:

The Solidarity Union's first head office was in Gdańsk-Wrzeszcz in a townhouse at 13 Marchlewskiego (now Dmowskiego) St. Photograph taken 1 September 1980.

(...) the next day we met in Wrzeszcz at 21 Marchlewskiego St. (...) we already go there, well, maybe not all of us, because there isn't enough room. (...) That was a mistake with that house... our headquarters, where we are to meet. It isn't 21, it's 13 (ridiculous). Thirteen. We should correct this! Thirteen. Maybe unlucky, maybe good – we'll see... [ZRG]

The provisional office for the organising Inter-Factory Founding Committee of the Independent Self-Governing Trade Union (not yet named "Solidarity") was procured by Gdańsk Voivode (Governor) Jerzy Kołodziejski. It was a multi-room apartment on the second floor of a 1904 townhouse at 13 Marchlewskiego St., which ran from Grunwaldzka Ave. (the chief road running through Gdańsk) to the railway station in Wrzeszcz. It was a peculiar historical irony that the budding trade union committee fighting for freedom against the communist authorities would install itself in a street named after Julian Marchlewski, an opponent of Poland's independence, co-founder of the Communist International, placed by Lenin in charge of the Provisional Revolutionary Committee of Poland in Białystok during the Bolshevik invasion of Poland in 1920. In ten years, after the fall of communism, the street would get a new patron – Roman Dmowski, who was among those who strove to achieve Poland's independence in 1918 and the founder of Poland's National Democratic Party.

The apartment belonged to a well-known Gdańsk doctor who saw his patients there. After the doctor left for abroad, the apartment remained empty. The regulations at the time strictly determined how many square metres a citizen could expect to receive from the state. And since the apartment was huge, there wasn't a big enough family in Gdańsk to fill it.

On 1 September, someone hung out a white and red flag. Just after ten o'clock a stream of people started to flood in. The rooms filled up, the floor squeaked but the wooden boards held. The queue of people grew until it spilled out into the street. It became apparent that a soon-to-be ten million strong trade union could not function in such conditions.

New address: Hotel Morski, 103 Grunwaldzka Ave.

Soon there was a new address, near the old one. Also in Wrzeszcz, but in Grunwaldzka Ave., the main throughway not only of Wrzeszcz, but of all Gdańsk. It was in the building of the former Hotel Morski, built in the 1960s. The ground floor had the Ster Shipyard Club, and above it was a hotel for the representatives of firms co-operating with the Shipyard, chiefly from the USSR. With time, the hotel ceased to meet the firms' requirements, so it was allotted as a hostel for nurses.

In the basement was one of the first gas cigarette lighter filling stations in town. (They may have been disposable in the West, but became refillable in the East.) At the front was the Sasanka flower shop with a doughnut shop right next to it, and there was a fur shop in the courtyard. On the left was the Neptun Department Store. Those who were not satisfied with what socialist commerce had to offer could go to the right to the Peweks shop which operated according to so-called "internal export" principles, where one could buy capitalist-made goods unavailable at Neptun for hard currency or special currency vouchers. Underneath it was a restaurant serving Russian cuisine, called Newska as a token of friendship between Gdańsk and Leningrad (which today is St Petersburg again). Looming over the area was a tower block with the Olimp cafe on its highest floor and another Peweks on its first floor. The tower block was commonly called the "dollar block", because when it was built some of the apartments could be purchased for dollars or other foreign currencies. In those days those who had hard currency could quickly get almost anything they wanted. In the internal export shops were plenty of black market money changers. They offered to exchange your zlotys into hard currency without the limits that were in force in the state bank. Or you could sell your hard currency at a much better exchange rate than the bank offered. However, such transactions required caution. One had to mind not only the money changer, but also the secret policemen hanging about...

Initially, the budding trade union took up the fifth floor of the hotel. The balcony of its leader's office overlooked Grunwaldzka Ave.

I liked that room in Grunwaldzka. It was right across from a long corridor and everyone coming there would finally come to me. It was a never-ending stream of people, cases, ideas and interventions. The idea of independent trade unions was a difficult sell in the rest of the country, so a great many people from all over Poland came to Gdańsk with reports, complaints and requests to intervene in their local communities, where the start of new organisations was often hindered. Gdańsk was to teach them, defend them, organise them and give them its mark. We became Poland's capital.
[DN]

On 17 September representatives of the independent trade union movement from the entire country assembled at the Ster club. They were to decide on the organisational form of the new movement. A decision which was fundamental not only for the movement itself, but also for Poland as a whole. The sessions were dramatic. Many representatives from smaller towns looked to battle-tested Gdańsk for help; they were afraid of difficulties during the court registration of their trade unions and thought that it would be easier to act together.

The Gdańsk people led by Wałęsa were sceptical. They knew each other practically inside-out and were a very tight group, while the people from the other parts of the country were practically unknown to them. The Gdańskers were afraid that the others might include careerists, people with ties to the authorities and security service agents who would weaken the movement. They were also afraid that a large organisation would become centralised and bureaucratised.

The motion that we should register as a single national structure was put forward by lawyer Jan Olszewski, an advisor from Masovia. He was seconded by Wrocław representative Karol Modzelewski. (...) According to Modzelewski, "Gdańsk won the day for us all. But we should not forget that it won thanks to the strong strike support of the entire country. The Coast will commit suicide if it breaks free from the rest of Poland." The decision was taken to form a single union. Modzelewski's motion to name it the Solidarity Independent Self-Governing Trade Union was passed. [SJH]

Simultaneously, the National Co-ordinating Commission with Chairman Lech Wałęsa was established.

The 17th of September is a peculiarly symbolic date in Poland's history. On that day in 1939 the Red Army invaded Poland, in 1980 the Solidarity Union was formed, while in 1993 the Russian Army left Poland.

It was here in the Ster Club that the National Co-ordinating Commission (KKP) and the Inter-Factory Founding Committee (MKZ) usually held their sessions, but for the most important sessions they would move to the BHP Hall at the Shipyard. Next door was the Union's print shop. Flags flapped and banners hung from the building. People used to gather there in search of independent information. And quilts and eiderdowns would air on the balconies in the rear of the building, because regular people still lived there.

The office in 103 Grunwaldzka Ave. operated until 13 December 1981, when martial law was enacted. The sight after the ZOMO[7] raid was staggering. The doors were broken in with axes or crowbars, closet doors and desk locks were broken, documents were all over the floor...

Part of the documentation was taken off by the authorities. It was likely then that the original copy of the historic Gdańsk Agreement of 31 August 1980 was lost.

Solidarity's second head office, Hotel Morski in Wrzeszcz in 103 Grunwaldzka Ave. The Union took up only part of the building; on the left balcony on the first floor one can see the bedding of the hotel's inhabitants drying. L. Wałęsa had his office on the 5th floor, on the left side with a fragment of his balcony visible in the picture. On the ground floor was the Ster Club, where the Union's executive would hold its sessions. At the front was the Sasanka flower shop. Today this building looks completely different. It houses a branch office of PKO BP S.A. Bank. Photograph from autumn 1980.

Later, the place becomes the office of the Voivode's Receiver for Union Property. Following the formal liquidation of Solidarity, the authorities moved in new tenants. Some moved in on their own. The building grew increasingly squalid. Burglaries, even arson attempts took place.

In the mid-1990s the old Hotel Morski was purchased by PKO BP Bank. As one of the largest organisations in Poland, the Bank carried out major renovation

[7] ZOMO – the communist regime's paramilitary riot police.

and opened its branch office No. 1 in Gdańsk there. Today, the building looks completely different. A floor was added, the balconies, from which banners were hung and on which quilts used to air, were walled off. The building's grey walls were replaced with a modern white and navy blue facade, reminiscent in its form of the Gdańsk Crane. The entrance through which Wałęsa passed on his way to the fifth floor is no more. There are lifts, which were not there at the time. The interior has changed as well. ATMs are in the place where the Sasanka flower shop once stood. The Ster Club, where Union members once deliberated about the future of Solidarity and Poland in clouds of cigarette smoke, has been turned into an operating room for the bank's customers, and what used to be the printing shop is now the operating room's back room. On the fifth floor, where Wałęsa and friends stood up for the due rights of their compatriots, now is the Restructuring and Vindication Centre in Warsaw, Branch Office in Gdańsk – an agency which stands up for what is due to the bank.

Unfortunately, there are no plaques to commemorate Solidarity's historical headquarters in 103 Grunwaldzka Ave. and 13 Dmowskiego St.

The entire neighbourhood has changed as well. More banks have moved in. The former Neptun, which for several years operated as the Centrum Shopping Centre, is practically deserted. The doughnut shop is no more. There is no more internal export which went the way of the money changers. The Newska restaurant is now open only on the ground floor. The Olimp cafe on top of the "dollar block" has disappeared altogether.

The Church in the Gdańsk district of Przymorze, 1 Najświętszej Maryi Panny Square

In the difficult days in the beginning of Solidarity, Wałęsa looked for motivation and strength for the new stage of life which awaited him. He found his confessor, Father Franciszek Cybula in the Church of the BVM Queen of the Holy Rosary. He had met him many years before, when he was preparing to marry Danuta.

I found a path for myself, which led through the Church, through religion, which I discovered for good during the difficult moments of the strike. It was the surest path in my life.

In the morning before breakfast, regardless of the time I went to sleep, I would go to the morning mass to the church in Przymorze – the one that Lenarciak built after December 1970. [DN]

When Wałęsa became President, he took Father Cybula with him to Warsaw, to the Belvedere[8]. Father Cybula would be Wałęsa's confidant and loyal friend during his difficult presidency.

The church, commonly known as the Okrąglak (Rotunda) for its round shape, was rather unceremoniously integrated into the apartment block development of Przymorze, a new housing district in Gdańsk. Previously churches were not foreseen in "modern housing estates." This one was built as an exception to socialist housing assumptions. Even though the local parish was established here in 1958, it was not until after December '70 that a church could be built. This was one of the few positive results of the meeting between the strikers and the new First Secretary of the Party. Henryk Lenarciak, Wałęsa's colleague from Dept. W-4, raised the issue of building a church in the centre of the housing estate which was being built at the time; Gierek promised and Lenarciak saw to it that he kept his word.

The Church of the BVM Queen of the Holy Rosary in the Gdańsk district of Przymorze. It was here that after August 1980 Lech Wałęsa went to mass every morning and found his confessor in Father Franciszek Cybula. This church in a new Gdańsk housing estate could only be built after December '70. This was one of the few positive results of the meeting between the strikers and the new First Secretary of the Party. Henryk Lenarciak, Wałęsa's colleague from the Shipyard, was among those who led to its construction.

[8] Then the seat of the President of the Republic of Poland.

The Monument to the Fallen Shipyard Workers, Solidarity Square

The Monument was the clearest and most obvious strike demand, prophesised and awaited like the Messiah in the Gospel. Henryk Lenarciak turned to Czesław Miłosz, laureate of the Nobel Prize for Literature, who then lived in Berkeley, California, to write a motto to place on the Monument. Miłosz sent a fragment of Psalm 29 in his translation:

"The LORD will give strength unto his people; the LORD will bless his people with peace."

The Shipyard workers and the designer of the Monument, Shipyard engineer Bogdan Pietruszka, added a fragment from another poem by Miłosz:

"You who have harmed a simple man,
Laughing at his wrongs...
Do not feel safe. The poet remembers.
The words are written down, the deed, the date."

Bogdan Pietruszka puts it bluntly: "The Monument was like a harpoon stuck in the body of a whale. The beast might thrash and fight, but our Monument shall remain..."

At the beginning of the strike Wałęsa took a wooden cross, which used to hang on the gate, from the Shipyard. The cross was cemented in the spot foreseen for the monument. Within a few months, a monumental, seventy metre high stature was erected. Forever.

The amount of trouble we had to get approval for the design! The Minister of Culture, a professor of architecture, was delegated to negotiate with us; he was simply pathetic when he ineptly began trying to get us to turn a design full of meaning and clear symbolism into something conventional, enigmatic, which would serve to blur the meaning. This was a clear frontline, where everyone had to show their stance and arguments and subject them to assessment. We were able to win on these frontlines, acquiring allies even in regime circles. [DN]

In the 1980s the official propaganda of the Polish People's Republic stubbornly called Solidarity Square "Workers' Solidarity Square".

Cross commemorating the Shipyard workers killed in December '70, placed in front of Gdańsk Shipyard's Gate No. 2 in the first days of the strike of August 1980. Later, on 16 December 1980, the Monument to the Fallen Shipyard Workers was unveiled nearby. The cross was moved to St Bridget's Church.

*The unveiling of the Monument to the Fallen Shipyard Workers.
The workers at the Shipyard demanded that their fallen colleagues
be commemorated after the December tragedy, as did the democratic
opposition in the late 1970s. This was one of the demands of the strikers
in 1980. The Monument's concept was presented by Shipyard designer
Bogdan Pietruszka already during the strike. The Monument's unveiling
on 16 December 1980 turned into a great patriotic demonstration.
Following the enactment of martial law, numerous demonstrations
in support of the underground Solidarity took place here in the 1980s.
The Monument is 42 metres high.*

Olivia Hall, Grunwaldzka Ave. The 1st Solidarity Trade Union National Assembly of Delegates

Olivia Hall, which stands in Grunwaldzka Ave., the main route which links Gdańsk with Sopot and further with Gdynia, was at the time the Tri-City's largest and most prestigious sport facility. The artificial skating rink, home ice of the Stoczniowiec Shipyard Hockey Club, was the stage for large-scale entertainment events, the most memorable of which was the "Soviet Circus," whose posters were all over town in December 1981...

The 1st Solidarity Trade Union National Assembly of Delegates in session at Olivia Hall in the autumn of 1981. L. Wałęsa is elected chairman. The delegates pass a "Message to the Working People of Eastern Europe" which would prove alarmingly prophetic for communism, as it turned out after less than a decade.

At the Assembly, Professor Father Józef Tischner presented assumptions of Solidarity ethics – the philosophical and ethical premises of the Solidarity civic movement. The main theme of the Assembly, however, was the campaign for the election of the Union president. Also appearing was a prophetic declaration of a "Message to the Working People of Eastern Europe," which at that time was very alarming for communism. The Olivia was teeming with Union life. Following a tempestuous debate, Wałęsa was elected president. He had great power over the Union; he was the de facto unquestioned head of a great civic movement.

For me, the set of resolutions and messages was purely theoretical. What really counted was only whether we could make a permanent "triple" arrangement between the regime, the Church and Solidarity. (...) Someone got really offended when I admitted once that I didn't know the details of a rather broad draught of the programme resolution. [DN]

Aeroplane at Gdańsk-Wrzeszcz Airport. The airport here was established after World War I. In the autumn of 1922, the planes of Poland's first regular airline came here. The airline was serviced by the Aerolloyd Company with Junkers F-13 aeroplanes which flew once a day on the Gdańsk-Warsaw-Lvov route. The last plane left here on 30 March 1974. This photograph was taken in 1949.

17 D Pilotów St. Apt. 3, 2nd Floor, Gdańsk Zaspa

As regards family matters, there was a major event: soon after signing the Agreement with the authorities, the Wałęsas moved from Stogi to Zaspa. The already eight-person family's new address was on the second floor of an eight-floor block of flats in a new housing estate.

Zaspa means dune in the Kashubian language. To the north it stretches to the seashore and Brzeźno, to the east and south it borders Wrzeszcz, and Przymorze to the west. Several dozen years ago this part of Gdańsk looked completely different. Gardens blossomed, even grain rustled amidst the sparse single-floor developments here. The neighbourhood's most characteristic spot was the Gdańsk-Wrzeszcz airport, which was established after World War I on the site of a former military airfield from 1910. In the autumn of 1922 the planes of Poland's first regular airline came here. The airline was serviced by the Aerolloyd Company with Junkers F-13 aeroplanes which flew once a day on the Gdańsk – Warsaw – Lvov route. In the autumn of the tragic year of 1939 thirty-eight defenders of the Polish Post Office in the Free City of Gdańsk were executed here. The postal workers and other victims of Nazism are buried at the cemetery on the edge of the neighbourhood.

In the late 1960s a decision was made to move the airport and to build a new large housing estate here. The last plane left here on 30 March 1974. A dozen or so weeks later, the first inhabitants moved into one of the buildings in Pilotów St. Żwirki i Wigury, Hynka, Burzyńskiego, Bajana, Skarżyńskiego, Dywizjonu 303 – the street names commemorate the biggest Polish flying aces. In the middle of this enormous housing estate, built in the cookie-cutter fashion of prefabricated concrete as everything was during Gierek's regime, remains a long runway, clearly separated from the development.

Old Gdańskers might tell you that the reason why dense housing was not sited in Zaspa before World War II was because of the groundwater flows here which purportedly adversely impact human health.

For the Wałęsas, however, the new address was a fantastic turn of events...

Bogdan Wałęsa

We kids lived and breathed our move to the new flat. It was something new and surprising, given the living conditions in Stogi with a tiny kitchen and two rooms. Our parents slept in the larger room. When Magda was born she slept with them. All four of us boys slept in the other smaller room. I can still remember well how the four of us would sleep in a single bed! There was a great big closet next to the bed. There was no room to move... [BW]

Gdańsk-Zaspa. The sprawling prefabricated concrete housing estate was built in the 1970s in place of the former Wrzeszcz airport. The old runway is visible in the foreground. The Wałęsas moved to Zaspa soon after the strike in 1980.

After many years of waiting, writing applications for the allotting of a larger apartment which would meet the requirements of the growing family, (...) the flat was allotted by the Gdańsk Voivode overnight. His direct motive was likely the reports by Western journalists, who were interested in me and my family and came to Stogi, where they saw, covered and filmed the life of six children within a little over a dozen square metres. That must have done the trick, too much even: I got an offer to move to a villa in fashionable Sopot. I told them, "No, thanks," I just wanted what I deserved according to the current Polish housing regulations, that is about ten square metres per person. Overnight, they emptied out the office of the housing co-op in Zaspa, joined the rooms with a corridor extension and that's how our flat came about. For us it seemed like a palace compared to what we'd had before. Incidentally, when my two other daughters, Maria Wiktoria and Brygida were born, and the largest room became the de facto office of Solidarity, the flat again became too small and it got crowded again. [DN]

And how does Danuta Wałęsa remember this event?
Was it a turn of events for her too?

*I believe it was on 4 September that they moved us to our
new flat in Zaspa. We wanted to switch from the flat in
Stogi to a larger apartment even before August. When
someone would place an ad wanting to swap, my husband
would go and ask. But then the Security Service would
arrive on the scene and there was no flat to swap anymore.*

*I said that "they moved us" because in fact it wasn't us who
moved out – they moved us. No one gave me any notice.
All of a sudden a car comes around, we pack and drive
off just as we stood. I had hot soup in the pot and I took
that soup to Zaspa.*

*After the strike I suppose the authorities were ashamed that
a person with such a large family lived in such a cubbyhole,
so they quickly found those quarters for us. We didn't get them
for free. We paid all the necessary money to the housing co-op.*

*The office was neglected and dirty. The rooms we moved
into with our small children were being repaired by a team
of construction workers all the time. From dawn to late
evenings the place was teeming with union people, advisers,
politicians, journalists and lunatics. One gentleman later
boasted that he had eaten a tasty dish of scrambled eggs at
the Wałęsas' home at seven in the morning. And there I was
having to take care of Ania, who was only a few months old,
and the other kids! It all became harder and harder for me
to take. One fine morning, I couldn't take it any more and
really kicked up a row with my husband in front of all those
people. And I was right, too. My husband got up and left
without a word. He came back after a few hours and said
that we should write on the door: "Typhoid.
No strangers allowed."*

Danuta Wałęsa looking out of the window of their apartment in Zaspa in 17 D Pilotów St.

*That left us with only each other, the children and
the construction workers. It was at least so calm that no
one else could come in. It was then that something broke
down inside me and I was really affected by all those radical
changes. Earlier, ever since our wedding in 1969, as a family
we were as tight as a clenched fist. A real hearth and home.
Self-reliant and independent. Then in Zaspa it dawned
on me that together with the birth of Solidarity all that had
disappeared. I knew that the life of our family would never
again be as it had been for eleven years.* [DW]

*Tanks in the vicinity of the Gdańsk Shipyard, on strike after the enactment
of martial law, most likely 15 December 1981. In the background
we can see the building of the Northern Regional Management
of the State Railway.*

The BHP Hall in December 1981, one more time...

Martial law changed all personal perspective.

When military couriers in Warsaw delivered notification of an extraordinary session of the Council of State, a two-day session of the Solidarity's National Commission was ending in Gdańsk. [DN]

The Commission's final session took place on 12 December 1981 at the BHP Hall; it had gone back to its roots. But General Jaruzelski's tanks were already rolling out on the cities' streets. The brittle and shaky arrangement between society and the authorities based on the Agreements signed in the Gdańsk Shipyard's BHP Hall, and which showed the way to make difficult changes, came crumbling down.

It was close to midnight. I did not take the floor. Only during the break in the sessions did I explain to journalists yet again the meaning of the words about confrontation which I had spoken in Radom. In this way I took issue with the official propaganda that had been going on in recent days. "When we speak of confrontation, we mean the force of arguments," I said, "We do not have and do not want to use physical force; we have no tanks and don't want them. Our words are simple and although they might sound brutal, the authorities should look to our intentions and not turn our words against us." (...) We didn't have the slightest chance of avoiding martial law. The slightest. Martial law was being prepared for a long time. By then they were only looking for a reason (...) Over all those months [from August 1980 to December 1981], I dedicated all my efforts to consolidate the situation which arose thanks to the August Agreements when Solidarity became a real civic movement and all of Poland cast off the torpor it had been in for many years. Did we lose in the end? Just think about it: after all, we won 500 days! [DN]

The police's "photographic documentation of security equipment damaged during street incidents in Gdańsk on 16–17 Dec. 1981." After pacifying the strike at the Gdańsk Shipyard on 16 December 1981, there were three days of fighting in the Gdańsk streets, in which several dozen thousand people took part.

On the night of 13 December, several thousand Solidarity people, including Wałęsa, were imprisoned in internment camps. From then on Gdańsk would stubbornly demand the release of the imprisoned and during skirmishes with the ZOMO riot police the chants, "Free Lech, imprison Wojciech!" rang out in the streets. And so it went on until Wałęsa was released.

Danuta Wałęsa

On 1 May 1982 thousands of people marched to my apartment block. I hung out a beach towel with the Solidarity logo from the balcony. The crowd chanted and cheered in honour of my husband. I recorded it all and took the cassette when I went to visit him. The visiting room was bugged. When he turned on the tape recorder and heard the cassette, he was happy and heartened. But I had problems. They searched me. I was with little Marysia, they searched the child's things, including the diapers. And they found the cassette. [DW]

Zaspa – the flat in Pilotów St. becomes the Union's office

On 10 November 1982, after almost a year of isolation, Wałęsa returned to Zaspa. A new, long stage begins. A team of advisers forms and an increasingly clearer strategy for non-violent fight for freedom is developed. This strategy will soon be appreciated by the Free World...

The office of the president of the outlawed Union was in his apartment. The day's work included the writing of statements, developing political ideas; in effect, it was a tough dialogue with the official propaganda. The apartment was under full surveillance. The flat was bugged and the telephone was bugged. A car with secret policemen inside stood at the door to the stairwell. Everyone who entered or exited was checked and recorded.

Demonstration in front of the Wałęsas' home in Zaspa on 1 May 1982. Lech Wałęsa was interned at the time. Two thousand people took part in the official May Day march organised by the communist authorities, while well over a dozen thousand demonstrators came to Zaspa.

*On 13 Nov. 1982, on the order of the Head of Department
B of the Voivodeship Command of the Citizens' Police
in Gdańsk, the secret external observation of citizen
Lech WAŁĘSA, code name "Ox", resident of Gdańsk-Zaspa
has commenced... The observed is the former chairman of
the NSZZ Solidarity National Commission (...) The goal
of the observation is to monitor the subject's behaviour,
the addresses he visits, determining the persons he comes
in contact with and determining the visitors to the subject's
residence. (...) The observation is to be carried out by
intelligence agents in a four-shift system (round the clock).
Three radio cars are to be used in the observation operation .
A signalling point has been organised in a private apartment
in order to ensure the correct surveillance of the subject and
the secrecy of the observation group (...)
Apart from the signalling point a hiding place for the
intelligence agents has been organised at (...). As the subject
resides in a stairwell where the offices of the Housing Co-op
are located, resulting in very many people visiting, we have
come into contact with Department T of the local Police
Command, which will signal every exit of persons from
the apartment of the observed. The following radio and
photographic equipment shall be used in the observation: two
radiotelephones, 9 personal radiotelephones, 3 photographic
cameras in different camouflage and binoculars. (...)*

*11 May 1983 contact – (...) vehicle – Mercedes van, Licence
No. W- 17 03, members of PERFECT rock band: 1.
Konarzewski Krzysztof, son of Witold and Celina, born on
(...), resident of Warsaw Mokotów (...); 2. Hołdys Zbigniew,
son of Henryk and Albina, born on (...), resident of Warsaw
Wola (...); 3. Kowalski Jarosław, son of Kazimierz and
Alfreda, born on (...), resident of Warsaw Praga (...);
4. Tarakowski Janusz, son of Czesław and Janina, born
on (...), resident of Warsaw Mokotów (...). [IPN]*

But there are also regular, pleasant things – Zaspa
becomes a tightly integrated community, one can get
underground literature under the counter at the kiosk

at Mr Doughnut, the Wałęsas go to their neighbour's parties. The May Day celebrations become mass demonstrations. Foreign TV crews come to Pilotów St. for improvised press conferences, and well-known personalities come to visit. The roster of stars could be surprising: Elton John in a cowboy hat, who came just to shake Wałęsa's hand; Joan Baez, with guitar, played a concert on the sofa under the picture of the Pope; famous piano duo Marek & Wacek; Lucjan Kydryński; the Perfect rock band.

"Visual material," i.e. a photograph of Lech Wałęsa, for the purposes of the agents of Department B of the Security Service, who on 13 November 1982, after he was released from internment, began his round-the-clock surveillance. His surveillance code names were "Poseidon", "Ox" and "Zenith."

Not all of the guests were nice. Once, one of the journalists opened the refrigerator without asking. He inspected the shelves and, either with interest, surprise or sneeringly remarked, "Oh, kielbasa!" Some time later there was a report on Poland, Gdańsk and of course about Wałęsa in one of the Western newspapers, where there was the following comment: "Perhaps it is not so bad in this country oppressed by communists, where the Solidarity freedom movement was outlawed, whose economy has wilted and needs the help of the West, since the workers' leader eats kielbasa every day."

Up and down – as if on a great big, overcrowded, crazy pneumatic see-saw – that is what this period of Wałęsa's work was like in Zaspa.

Wałęsa's office, although organised in impromptu fashion and operating with few people, was like the mini-ministry of a non-existent government. This government held open dialogue, which fortunately was appreciated abroad.

The Nobel Peace Prize
Pilotów St., 5 October 1983

He returned home about half past five. The people in Gdańsk already knew; the street greeted Lech enthusiastically, with fingers showing the V sign. Father Henryk Jankowski awaited him in the road by the allotment gardens. Father Jankowski was beginning to grow irritated: people had been gathering since morning, and by now there was a big crowd; lots of police; Danusia's head was swimming, foreign journalists were constantly calling. "We have to quickly figure out what we are to do with this Prize."... The company which returned with Wałęsa from mushroom picking in the forest burst out with laughter. Wałęsa replied, "I've figured it out."

Journalists in front of the Wałęsas' apartment block in Zaspa in 17D Pilotów St. awaiting Lech Wałęsa. First half of the 1980s.

He came home; in a moment, he stood in the window:

*"I believe that this is our joint Prize, an appreciation
of all of us, who want to move forward in a non-violent
way through agreement. I feel that since others understand
us – smart people, perhaps smarter than we are, their
economy and lifestyle certainly go to show for it –" (the crowd
laughs and applauds) "then sooner or later we will also
be appreciated in our own country, where for the time being
we are being deprived of what we deserve. I am convinced
that we will sit down at the table and come to an agreement
for the good of Poland...*

*As regards the material side of our joint Prize, I have
decided to give it to the Polish Episcopate, who we all trust,
they are a reliable firm, for the Agricultural Development
Fund. We've all got to eat...* [NdW]

*The awarding of the Nobel Prize put me in the company of
persons who have got their own statues. But I didn't want
to be a hero. I neither wanted to be a statue, nor a saint.
I preferred the skin of a pragmatic politician, who tried to
unwind or cut the Polish knot. I never thought of becoming
another wax figure in the vanquished heroes' cabinet.
The years that were ahead required more of a fox than a lion.*
[DdW]

Wałęsa took his Nobel Peace Prize Medal to Jasna
Góra, the Mountain of Light in Częstochowa, as
a votive offering. The money, which he wanted to
donate to a Church foundation supporting Poland's
rural areas, never got to that institution. The authorities
piled up problems and eventually the money was spent
on the purchase of equipment for the Shipyard hospital.

June 1987 – John Paul II comes to Gdańsk

There were attempts to organise a visit of John Paul II, the spiritual father of the movement, to Gdańsk, the birthplace of Solidarity, before. It had not been possible.

The former Metropolitan of Gdańsk, Archbishop Tadeusz Gocłowski, who consistently supported Wałęsa and Solidarity's mission, was a witness to those moments:

(...) The communists not only knew their history, but also knew well that something was going on here, that something persisted and might explode. They absolutely did not want to agree to the Pope's visit to Gdańsk also in 1987. What is more, I can even say that it was as if the Church was understanding of this. It was in 1986, I believe, that Archbishop Dąbrowski and I were at the Vatican. I brought a letter which officially invited the Pope to visit Gdańsk. Toward the end of our dinner, Father Dziwisz[9] put the letter on the table between the Pope and myself. The Holy Father said, "I don't have to read it, I know what's in it. Gocłowski's inviting me to Gdańsk." Archbishop Dąbrowski then said, "Your Holiness, it is still impossible this time...". The Pope fell silent. There was a long silence, which seemed to last an eternity. At last the Pope spoke, "Right Revered Archbishop, if I were not to come to Gdańsk yet again, I would rather think whether to go to Poland at all, because then I would be used as a tool by the communist system." I thought to myself then, "Holy Father, you're a great man." After coming back to Poland, Archbishop Dąbrowski got in touch with the communist authorities and told them that if they wanted the Pope in Poland, he had to come to Gdańsk. That was a sine qua non condition. Of course, later there was a struggle as to the agenda. The authorities did everything they could to keep the Pope away from the Monument to the Shipyard Workers killed in 1970.

---

[9] Private secretary to Pope John Paul II. Now the Archbishop of Cracow.

12 June 1987, a forest of banners with support for the underground Solidarity appears above the heads of the people greeting John Paul II in the Gdańsk district of Zaspa.

Even the Episcopate spokesman Father Alojzy Orszulik tried to convince me, "Just absolutely leave it alone, don't destroy the Pope's agenda. Let the Pope bless the Monument from afar." I replied, "No. If the Pope is in Gdańsk, if he's passing by the Monument, he must come up to the Monument and to the Shipyard." It was only my personal letter to the Pope with my proposed agenda that helped. The Pope signed off on all the points: Zaspa, Westerplatte, St Mary's Church and of course the Monument at the Shipyard, so that there were no doubts and no going back.

When the Pope rode up to the Shipyard Workers' Monument, the communists, not wanting to allow people there, brought several thousand apparatchiks and Security Service agents who stood with their backs to the Pope. It was a desperate gesture of communist stupidity. There was absolute silence by the Monument, while all over Gdańsk there were shouts of joy and enthusiasm. The Pope said then, "There is a shout in this silence." [TG]

Visit of former American president Ronald Reagan to Gdańsk in September 1990. R. Reagan salutes Poland's Solidarity in front of the Monument to the Fallen Shipyard Workers next to Gdańsk Shipyard's Gate No. 2.

Two years later, already after the first partially free elections, George H.W. Bush, the then President of the United States, came to the Monument, where he announced the beginning of a strategy of financial aid, which would support the economic transformations in Poland, and together with Wałęsa raised his arm high with the victory sign. In September 1990, former US President Ronald Reagan visited with his wife Nancy, and saluted Wałęsa, Solidarity, Gdańsk and Poland. French President François Mitterrand arrived, as did other European leaders. Hollywood stars came, for instance Robert de Niro with Roman Polański...

For all of them this was an opportunity to meet and get a close look at a legend, who overthrew communism. Then, in the late 1980s, the route various VIPs would take when visiting Poland changed. Gdańsk became a permanent fixture.

After the breakthrough events, not only for Poland, of 1989, well known lawmakers and artists would come to Gdańsk. Under the Monument to the Fallen Shipyard Workers: (from left) Roman Polański, Robert de Niro and Gustaw Holoubek.

Wałęsa had become an icon and a point of reference of new European politics already in August 1980. Over the next ten years, without representing any official structure of the Polish People's Republic, he was the de facto ambassador of the new Poland, giving European and world leaders the opportunity to stand on the side of the new political order in Europe.

The Monument to the Fallen Shipyard Workers became a symbolic stage for this theatre of political gestures which provided an opportunity for heads of state to express their common ideals and meet the expectations of their constituents in an easier way than with binding treaties.

It was also therapeutic by paying back the moral debts of the history of the ideals of freedom betrayed after the Second World War for the satiation of their own societies and a relative level of military security in Europe.

After years of vulgar attacks in the press, radio and on television, they finally began to take us seriously. We stepped on the road to agreement. Sticking to our opinions and ideas we began to talk rather than fight. [IKJK]

Ship under construction: the Papal altar

Then, in June 1987, the empty space of the former runway of the airport in Zaspa became the site of the meeting of the people of Gdańsk and Poland with the Pope. A sea of banners written in characteristic Solidarity fonts sprang up above the million people gathered there. The atmosphere there was completely different than at the Monument just a moment before. An extraordinary grand altar in the form of a ship, designed by Marian Kołodziej, awaited the Pope.

The Ship Under Construction altar for Pope John Paul II, designed by Marian Kołodziej. In June 1987, John Paul II celebrated in Zaspa a memorable mass for the working people.

Meeting of Pope John Paul II with Lech Wałęsa at the Gdańsk Curia.
5 June 1999.

"I speak to you and in a sense for you."
And then came the homily with its most important motto:
"Carry each other's burdens, not one against the other's."
[JDBN]

Archbishop Gocłowski remembers:

The Pope loved Gdańsk, loved Solidarity and knew well
what it stood for. He was a man who had a fantastic
vision about Solidarity's value as a movement which was
to have an impact on Europe. He was perfectly aware of
this. It was apparent that communism was badly wounded.
It was first wounded by the Pope's election, then with his
first pilgrimage to Poland in 1979. When he stepped up on
the ship-altar in Zaspa, the Pope said, "This is a ship under
construction." That was a clear suggestion. The mood formed
itself. The organisers wanted to force the Pope to sit behind
a bullet-proof pane away from the people. And he said,
"Right reverend bishop, I go where the Bible is read, so I'm
going to the captain's bridge." And from that moment on,
the crowd was his. I was sitting beside Cardinal Casaroli.
He had the text of the Pope's homily in Italian, I didn't.
Every now and again a burst of incredible applause would
come. The mood infected Casaroli, who began to respond.
Reading the text, he would tell me, "Here we go again."
[TG]

In 1999, Gdańsk painter Rafał Roskowiński, known
for his monumental murals, painted another one.
This time on the gable wall of the apartment block in
Dywizjonu 303 St. The mural commemorates the people
who have made a special mark on the history of Zaspa.
It depicts John Paul II and Lech Wałęsa.

Mural by Rafał Roskowiński
on the wall of an apartment
block in Dywizjonu 303 St.
The mural commemorates
John Paul II and
Lech Wałęsa, two people who
have made a special mark
on the history of Zaspa.

The Pope was the co-originator and promoter of the
Polish transformations: he supported the Polish cause
before the world and in the country itself before
the communist regime. Years later, when the crisis
of difficult freedom came and the ties of the former
unity were breaking, he was not emotional and nor was
he judgmental. During the final meeting at the Bishop's
Palace in Oliwa, when he was very tired after
the pilgrimage in 1999, he told Wałęsa,

"Mr Lech, what happened, happened!" [DAK]

St Bridget's Parish, 17 Profesorska St.

There are certain "cult" places in Gdańsk. The very
name of St Bridget arouses a stream of associations and
recollections relating to the history of contacts between
Poland and Scandinavia, but the most important are
the xrecollections associated with Solidarity. St Bridget's
is a special church and a special place; the parish priest
was Father Henryk Jankowski. During martial law
and in the years that followed it, St Bridget's was the
unofficial embassy of the outlawed Solidarity. Formally
speaking, St Bridget's is the Shipyard's parish church,
as it was the closest to the Gdańsk Shipyard, which is
why Father Jankowski was summoned by the Shipyard
workers during the strike in August 1980 to celebrate
a mass for the strikers. During the difficult years that
followed Wałęsa would meet here with the Solidarity
people. Writers, artists, musicians, journalists and
Solidarity activists from all over the country all
came here. For years, actors from Gdańsk and from
throughout Poland led by Daniel Olbrychski performed
here, reciting poetry which brought hope and strength.
After masses in the intention of the homeland,
improvised rallies and public press conferences were

held here by Wałęsa, after which the inspired crowd would often march to the Shipyard, heedless of the ZOMO units and their truncheons.

The "heralds of freedom" would come here from the West. Professor Zbigniew Brzeziński would come here from the United States to speak about the political directions the world was developing in. Senator Edward Kennedy and family and actress Jane Fonda and her congressman husband also showed their support. At dinner in the presbytery, the Iron Lady, British Prime Minister Margaret Thatcher, spoke these important words to Wałęsa:

"You've already made a few giant steps on the road to freedom. You are doing this out of moral conviction and that's why you'll never give up." [DdW]

Counter-march on 1 May 1983, which formed on Rajska St. after the crowd left St Bridget's Church. In the background, left, St Katherine's Church.

Crowd in the square in front of St Bridget's Church during mass for the homeland celebrated on the anniversary of the beginning of the August strike. 14 August 1983.

Archbishop Tadeusz Gocłowski remembered the splendid atmosphere of that meeting:

The way they, Thatcher and Wałęsa, would talk to each other as equals. And there was a crowd standing outside the window. She would listen and time and again would ask, "What are they shouting now?" "Down with Jaruzelski!", "Long live Solidarity!" "Oh, good," she would comment. The mood was perfect. Apart from the two central figures, at the table sat Geremek, Mazowiecki and Onyszkiewicz, who served as interpreter. On the following day I left for Rome. I gave the Pope a report on these talks and on the situation in Poland. [TG]

Father Jankowski, who is a well known gourmand, often made these meetings rather sumptuous affairs. At the dinner with Thatcher he served pheasant, which later became legendary. Rumour has it that Thatcher, when she saw the platters with pheasant being brought in, could barely contain her surprise. She came to the poor Poland of the 1980s, and here they served her pheasant...

Sometimes, the parties at the canon could take on a humorous twist. Once, at the conclusion of a lavish banquet, at which the economic crisis in Poland was one of the topics of conversation, Father Jankowski came in majestically with a gift. It was a large decorated plate. Turning to a VIP from abroad he said, "I hereby give you this commemorative plate as a symbol of our empty plates in Poland." Upon hearing these words, the guests couldn't stop themselves from laughing.

After those days of "Bridget's" glory, came, in the 1990s, the days of controversial doings by Father Jankowski. Many of those who would come here during the glory days would stop visiting him. Wałęsa himself, although Father Jankowski remains his friend, very rarely comes here anymore.

The Dominican Friars and the Church of St Nicholas, 72 Świętojańska St.

This church was one of the few churches in Gdańsk to survive the War almost unscathed, which is why we can marvel at its lavish interior. It was there that Andrzej Wajda shot scenes for *Man of Iron*, a film about the budding Solidarity, which received the Palme d'Or at the Cannes Film Festival in 1981 and was nominated for an Oscar. Anna Walentynowicz and Lech Wałęsa both played bit parts in the film.

The police's "photographic documentation of street incidents in Gdańsk on 31 August 1982 (damage)." The photograph shows the burnt vehicles of the Second Company of the Gdańsk Reserve Police Unit in Zwycięstwa Ave. The day was the second anniversary of August '80. Gdańsk was one of several large Polish cities which were the sites of the biggest demonstrations against the communist regime and the hardest street fights in the 1980s.

The Dominican Order, which St Nicholas' Church belongs to, certainly played an important role in the history of Gdańsk. In 1260, Pope Alexander IV granted indulgence to the Dominican Order on St Dominic's Day (August 4). The great number of pilgrims who would come to the fete to St Nicholas' Church led the Town Council to organise a fair. The tradition has survived throughout the centuries and today St Dominic's Fair brings millions of tourists into the city each summer. It is the largest, next to Munich's Oktoberfest, such event in Europe.

In the early 1970s, a Dominican Friar, Father Ludwik Wiśniewski, took a group of politically minded teenagers under his wing. They came mainly from Secondary School No. 1 and the Secondary School in Topolowa St. and would later become students at the University of Gdańsk, Gdańsk University of Technology and the Medical University. They were the ones who in a few years would form the Young Poland Movement.

During martial law and later, Father Sławomir Słoma organised a chaplaincy for artistic circles here and the Dominican basilica became a centre of artistic life in Gdańsk. Exhibitions of the banned Association of Polish Artists and Designers were organised and an independent gallery was set up in the vaults of the church. Poets and prose writers (some better, some worse) would give public readings. The writers ran "Speaking, Points", where they would present texts which could not be officially printed. Guests writers from all over Poland would come: Herbert, Szymborska, Kapuściński, Bratkowski, Fedorowicz, Father Tischner. The opposition was represented by Mazowiecki, Onyszkiewicz, Geremek, Wielowieyski and Celiński. Wałęsa would often drop by. The actors of the Wybrzeże Theatre would put on productions. In a word, the church was teeming with life: both openly dissident and less overt, subtle forms. At the university chaplaincy, in the rooms up in the attic, Wałęsa's biography The *Road of Hope* was written, later to be published in all the world's languages as his fullest authorised statement which explained the path, motives and biography of the leader of Solidarity.

Lech Wałęsa on the set of Man of Iron, directed by Andrzej Wajda.
Scene in St Nicholas' Church in Gdańsk with (from left)
Krystyna Janda, Jerzy Radziwiłłowicz and Anna Walentynowicz.
In 1981, the film won the Palme d'Or in Cannes.

One last time in the BHP Hall...

It was mainly young workers who went on strike at the Gdańsk Shipyard in May and August 1988. They were supported by striking students. But in comparison with August 1980 there were few people on strike, just a few hundred in the Shipyard itself, and no one really knew what it would lead to.

The strikers would once again "sleep on Styrofoam mats," and Wałęsa decided to get involved in this reckless, strange strike. In the BHP Hall, following the news from behind-the-scenes talks run by advisors and intermediaries, the decision came to take a risk – to negotiate with the regime, which ultimately led to the Round Table agreements.

And so the 3rd Polish Republic, with its partially free elections to the Sejm (the lower house of the Polish Parliament) and already free elections to the Senate, was born.

Before the communists, who had been ruling Poland since 1945, would suffer an ignominious defeat in the elections of 4 June 1989, the parliamentary candidates of the Solidarity Citizens' Committee came to the Shipyard like to a mother. The scenario is simple: a mandatory picture of Wałęsa to be placed on the campaign poster. Such advertising was all they needed. Poland's success in the June elections was almost 100% complete. That very same day, however, the communist system would show that it was still alive and kicking. Chinese tanks rolled over the students protesting in Tiananmen Square. Soon, however, communism would fall everywhere in Central and Eastern Europe: the "Autumn of Nations" came, the Berlin Wall fell, Germany united and the Soviet Union fell apart.

Solidarity's final head office, 24 Wały Piastowskie St.

The Union, legally re-established in 1988, needed a head office. The old one in Wrzeszcz was completely inadequate. A proposal was made to take over the Hotel Monopol building in what was then Gorki Square across from the main train station. The building was very squalid, however, and Solidarity had no money for the renovation and adaptation work.

Krzysztof Pusz, Wałęsa's then chief of staff, recalls how the search went on and on:

"Wałęsa would become irritated and make a fuss about not having anywhere to work, not to mention where to host the delegations which were arriving in increasing numbers."

View of the junction of Rajska and Wały Piastowskie Streets. On the right is the building of the Projmors Maritime Construction Design Office, where Solidarity has its head office today, on the left the Green Skyscraper, one of the most distinctive buildings in the Gdańsk city centre. Photograph from March 1968.

Eventually the Voivode decided to give Solidarity the building of the Projmors Maritime Construction Design Office, an enterprise which grew out of the Harbour Reconstruction Office in the centre of Gdańsk in 24 Wały Piastowskie St. The same building that the regime was to give to Solidarity right before the enactment of martial law! This large building was built in the 1950s as a head office for the Węglokoks coal and coke export enterprise. The building was built on a huge air-raid shelter, which towards the end of World War II also served as a field hospital. Today, the former air-raid shelter provisionally houses the Roads to Freedom exhibition. The building itself has the Akwen hall, which is where Solidarity's current authorities hold their sessions and whose name refers to the former Akwen club restaurant and disco which belonged to the Gdańsk Repair Shipyard.

In the spring of 1989, Wałęsa and the reborn Union received several rooms on the fifth floor in the rear of the building to begin with. Of course, it was not enough. That is why the Union president's office soon moved to the third floor, this time on the front side. He finally had the space to work and to host guests.

And there were so many of them that the doors would hardly ever close. Activists and regular people, artists and lawmakers, heads of important and less important organisations, ambassadors and nut-jobs.

In January 1990, the Soviet ambassador Vladimir Brovikov came to Gdańsk with an invitation for Wałęsa to visit his country. Wałęsa took advantage of the opportunity. Saying he had nothing to hide he told the clearly surprised Brovikov in front of the media about the painful Polish-Soviet relationship: about the historic necessity to quickly remove the Soviet Army from Poland, to accept the truth about the Katyn Massacre and the problem of compensation for those exiled to Siberia, and finally about the files of the Trial of the Sixteen[10]:

24 Wały Piastowskie St. This is how the head office of Solidarity looks like today. Formerly this building housed the Projmors Maritime Construction Design Office. The Union and L. Wałęsa moved in here in 1989.

"The system you built in Poland based on force and tanks is becoming a thing of the past. We must remember, however, that our nation is awaiting for answers to many issues, such as the invasion of 17 September 1939, the murder of twelve thousand Polish officers and intellectuals in Katyn, lack of free access to the places where our ancestors lie buried and where monuments of our culture stand.

To Brovikov's growing surprise Wałęsa then presented a vision of a new neighbourly relationship, "Poles will be able to visit formerly Polish lands, but that does not mean we want to change the borders."

Wałęsa spoke to the ambassador in a tenor which had been long awaited in Poland: conciliatory but clear:

"I know that you are going through internal problems, but if we are to arrive at a new way of doing things, then we need to talk in plain terms. And so far we have always been fighting for everything by force." [ANTY]

---

[10] A staged trial of 16 kidnapped leaders of the Polish Secret State in World War II held by the Soviet Union in Moscow in 1945.

When he was already the President of Poland, Wałęsa took the topic up again during his talks with Boris Yeltsin. On 17 September 1993, the final unit of the Russian Army left Poland, while earlier Yeltsin's special envoy Rudolf Pikhoya brought the most important part of the Katyn documents to the Belvedere.

When Wałęsa saw the document with Joseph Stalin's personal signature ordering the execution of thousands of Polish officers, he could not contain his emotion.

Several months after the ambassador's visit another important meeting took place. This time, it was confidential. The meeting was held not in Wały Piastowskie St., but in Oliwa at Archbishop Gocłowski's, who remembers it thus:

"I invited all the great politicians of the day. There was Wałęsa, Mazowiecki, Geremek, Olszewski, Michnik, Kuroń, Hall... ten people in all. I must admit that Wałęsa had no doubts that it was he who should become president. At the very beginning of the meeting, he said straight out, "I will be president." As if he had it all set. Then he added that Mr Mazowiecki, who was a great Prime Minister, should continue being the PM and that Mr Geremek, if he so wished, could become the Vice-President. And so he dealt the cards. Perfectly, in my opinion. I felt that Mazowiecki, who was a fantastic prime minister, should have continued that mission. While the leader of Solidarity, which turned the world upside down, should be the president.

But Mazowiecki said, "We'll fight for the presidency." I regretted that it didn't work out. I though that it was a good idea: let Mazowiecki remain Prime Minister, Geremek become Vice-President, and keep Wałęsa in charge of everything, but augmented with the intellect of Mazowiecki, Geremek and others. [TG]

And so the die was cast. On 9 December 1990 at the Akwen, on the victorious post-election evening, Wałęsa raised his famous toast, "To your health, in our throats."

Danuta and Lech Wałęsa on election night in the Gdańsk Akwen Club after the results of the Polish presidential election were announced on 9 December 1990. L. Wałęsa then raised the famous toast; "To your health, in our throats."

Gdańsk-Oliwa, 54 Polanki St. – Wałęsa's current address

After all those years, Wałęsa, a Gdańsker by choice, became the President of Poland and moved to the Belvedere in Warsaw. From then on he would visit Gdańsk as Poland's most important VIP. After some time, he announced that on weekends he would host foreign statespeople in his home town, in Gdańsk. We can see their pictures today in the vestibule which leads to Arthur's Court.

Before he became president, Wałęsa and his family moved to the Gdańsk district of Oliwa. This is a completely different neighbourhood from the monotonous Zaspa, a high-rise bedroom suburb. Oliwa's history is much richer as it dates back to the 12th century. It has a cathedral with a world-famous organ. It was here that the peace treaty following the Polish-Swedish War was signed in 1660. It was here that Gdańsk aristocrats would build their manors at the foot of the woody hills in Polanki St. beginning in the 17th century. One of these manors was the birthplace of the famous philosopher Arthur Schopenhauer. "It is one of the most beautiful places in Europe," is how the 18th century German traveller Alexander von Humboldt wrote about Oliwa.

In contemporary times, Oliwa and Gdańsk have acquired a university, a mosque (one of three in Poland) which serves the Polish Tartars who have settled in Gdańsk, and the St Bridget Ecumenical Centre. Unfortunately, it also acquired a lot of box-shaped villas. Still, when we walk along the streets of Oliwa, we can feel the atmosphere of old Gdańsk.

It was here that the Wałęsas moved into an old 120 square metre house with a large garden in 54 Polanki St. in 1988.

It was a bargain; the previous owner was leaving the country. First some necessary renovation and the family could move in.

A year later Wałęsa had dinner with George and Barbara Bush at the house:

The interpreter had an unenviable job (...), because President Bush and I constantly had something to say. My method of holding a conversation consisted in oscillating around the most important idea: so the world would help correlate political reforms with the economic reforms which had lagged behind. I emphasised that when meeting the head of a global superpower, I could expect co-operation with a target sum of 10 billion dollars. Of course, not in the form of loans, much less grants, but in the form of capital deposited in the great banks, to be drawn upon by Polish entrepreneurs. George Bush listened very carefully to this, then said that he liked that vision. And that he awaited a concrete suggestion for co-operation in various domains. [DdW]

Lech Wałęsa's house in 54 Polanki St. in Oliwa. The Wałęsas moved here from Zaspa in the summer of 1988. This photograph from spring 1989 shows the old house which was torn down after L. Wałęsa finished his term as President of Poland in 1995.

There is another anecdote tied to this particular visit. The renovation work on the Wałęsas' new home started before the visit. The agenda of the Bushes' visit included a walk around the vast garden. It so happened that the US President reached a distant part of the garden where a bathtub removed from the renovated bathroom stood. Never mind whether there was no time to send it to the scrap heap or whether it was to become a water tank for watering the garden. In any event, Bush Senior was to have asked whether his hosts liked to bathe outdoors.

The Wałęsas' house in 54 Polanki St. View from the garden.

The house in Polanki St. is completely different from the apartment in Zaspa for one other reason: a tight fence, a box with security people, cameras and high trees.

Our world has changed. Not always according to the scenario we or Wałęsa himself had expected.

It was at 54 Polanki St. that Wałęsa suffered the bitter defeat in the presidential elections of 1995. That was not the end of his problems. When he lost the election, the ruling Left remembered about a biopic on Wałęsa which was to be filmed by Warner Bros. Earlier, Wałęsa had received a million dollars for the rights. Ultimately, the film was not produced, but Wałęsa's opponents began to claim that he should pay taxes on the royalties. Upon the motion of the Tax Office, the court established a mortgage on the real estate in 54 Polanki St. This complex and controversial matter went on for months until the court finally decided that the Tax Office had no grounds to demand the payment from Wałęsa.

In place of the old house, Wałęsa finally built a new residence for this family. Some say that he himself sat in the driver's seat of the excavator preparing the construction site. The new house was designed by well-know Gdańsk architect Szczepan Baum.

Gdańsk's Millennium

1997 was the year of Gdańsk's Millennium. Any jubilee, especially a thousand-year jubilee, requires appropriate prestige. By now the time has come to disclose some behind-the-scenes events that took place then.

It is self-evident that for any city such an anniversary is a good opportunity to recall its many centuries of achievements and history. However, in Gdańsk's case the situation was made rather complex because of current political events. Gdańsk's most recognisable symbol was Lech Wałęsa, now the former President of Poland. The sitting president, however, was Aleksander Kwaśniewski from the Left, which also had control of the government. Wałęsa, who bore a grudge because of his recent electoral defeat, was not particularly fond of Kwaśniewski. But it was Kwaśniewski who was now president, and would certainly come if invited. But what would Wałęsa do?

The millennium was inaugurated in April with a ceremonial session of the Gdańsk City Council. Since this was a local parliamentary session, the current President of Poland was not invited; the Marshals of the Sejm and Senate were present though. Wałęsa was the guest of honour. Kwaśniewski sent a letter which was read at the session. Kwaśniewski, together with German President Roman Herzog, took part in another important part of the Millennium, the Convention of the New Hansa. This part of the agenda took place without Wałęsa.

To mark the occasion of Gdańsk's millennium, the former presidents of the United States (George Bush), Poland (Lech Wałęsa) and Germany (Richard von Weizsäcker) received honorary citizenship of the city on 30 June 1997. Here in the garden of Wałęsa's home in 54 Polanki St.

The Millennium was certainly a good reason to invite other well known persons from abroad to Gdańsk. In the early autumn of 1996, the then Chairman of the Gdańsk City Council (now Mayor) Paweł Adamowicz visited Wałęsa at his residence in Polanki St. The conversation was not an easy one, but Wałęsa gave free rein.

The formula for the invitations was clear and simple. Margaret Thatcher, who helped to overthrow communism when she was Prime Minister. Ditto George Bush. Germany was united during Richard von Weizsäcker's presidency. And, of course, Gdańsker by choice Lech Wałęsa. It was already known then that Ronald Reagan unfortunately would not be able to come for health reasons. François Mitterrand in turn, who although controversially he had hosted General Jaruzelski in 1985, after 1989 had strongly supported Poland in the matters of the reduction of its foreign debt and the final acceptance of the Polish-German border, was dead.

The biggest problems concerned Thatcher and Bush. When one could come, the other could not. When practically the final date arrived, it suddenly turned out that Thatcher was to represent the United Kingdom at the transfer of Hong Kong to China. It was too late. It couldn't be helped, the Iron Lady would have to accept her honorary citizenship later.

On 30 June 1997, the three former presidents sat down in Arthur's Court on Gdańsk chairs and Wałęsa, who had been sceptical just months before, became teary-eyed. Interestingly, George and Barbara Bush came from Warsaw to the celebrations in Gdańsk by train.

After the ceremonies, the already relaxed ex-presidents walked in the garden in 54 Polanki St.

The garden is the site of Wałęsa's grand birthday and name-day celebrations. It has become a political salon of sorts. Ever since Wałęsa and Kwaśniewski shook hands in Rome at John Paul II's funeral in 2005, the Kwaśniewskis have been coming over to Polanki for the name-day party. Other times, representatives of the full range of Poland's political spectrum appear.

Cristal Restaurant, Gdańsk-Wrzeszcz, 105 Grunwaldzka Ave.

For years, the menu, guest list and the ceremony of greeting all the more distinguished guests has been the duty of Ryszard Kokoszka, owner of the Cristal Restaurant in Wrzeszcz in 105 Grunwaldzka Ave., near what was Solidarity's second head office.

Kokoszka is a colourful character, who certainly has taken advantage of his friendship with the Wałęsas. He is a graduate of the Catering Academy in Budapest. In the 1970s he provided the catering for meetings between the heroes of socialist labour and First Secretary Edward Gierek and Prime Minister Piotr Jaroszewicz in Gdańsk Shipyard.

Kokoszka first met Wałęsa in August 1980, when he drove up to the striking Shipyard with his truck full of cakes and doughnuts.

At Cristal, Kokoszka organised the wedding and christening parties of Wałęsa's offspring. He is certainly a man of commercial and political vision. He organised the first and only World Liberals' Ball for the Liberal-Democratic Congress party. He also organised a team-building New Years' Eve Ball for the former ruling coalition of Solidarity Electoral Action and the Freedom Union. The hit of the night was "You Love Only Once," performed by Irena Jarocka and MP Henryk Wujec.

In those days Kokoszka was called the premier by his friends. The Left in turn would call his restaurant the Solidarity Electoral Action's cafeteria. At the Cristal, Kokoszka hosted Wałęsa's successor as President of Poland, Aleksander Kwaśniewski and his wife and many more distinguished lawmakers. It was customary for him to introduce dishes named for successive presidents and other well-known personalities into the menu. And so there was herring à la Wałęsa and à la Kwaśniewski, Prelate Jankowski's delicacy and spaghetti Krzaklewski.

The passage of time had left its mark on several of the VIPs and the same happened to the Cristal. Life moves on. Kokoszka sold his establishment to a bank. The Cristal would go on, but a little bit further away, and a little bit smaller.

The Cristal Restaurant and restaurant gardens in Grunwaldzka Ave. in Gdańsk-Wrzeszcz, May 1990. L. Wałęsa would hold many family, and even political functions in this restaurant.

The row after Grass's confession

In August 2006, the past once again caught up with
Gdańsk, Lech Wałęsa and many others on account
of an unexpected confession by Günter Grass, who told
about his service in the Waffen SS in the *Frankfurter
Allgemeine Zeitung*. World War II was drawing to
a close, he was seventeen years old and served in the
unit for only a short time without taking part in any war
crimes. But for years he remained silent on the matter.
He disclosed this just before the publication of his new
book, Peeling the Onion. After this confession of the
native-born Honorary Citizen of the City of Gdańsk
and winner of the Nobel Prize in Literature, all hell
broke loose. Accusations flew that Grass had hidden
the truth for too long, that by speaking about the SS
after all those years, he just wanted to generate publicity
for his new book. There were calls demanding that
Grass be deprived of his Honorary Citizenship.

Wałęsa, as a Pole, as a Gdańsker by choice and as
an Honorary Citizen of the City, was in a difficult
situation. What the Germans did during the War
had painfully affected Poles, including Wałęsa himself:
he had lost his father. He had forgiven, but he did
not forget.

"I'll give up my Citizenship, because I cannot be an
Honorary Citizen together with Grass. In Grass's place
I would give it up myself," was Wałęsa's knee-jerk
reaction. However, a while later he added, "I admire
him for his courage, for admitting after all those years,
but I still expect of him to make a gesture towards
the people of Gdańsk."

Gdańsker by choice Lech Wałęsa and Gdańsker by birth Günter Grass. The first is the winner of the Nobel Peace Prize of 1983, the latter received the Nobel Prize for Literature in 1999. On the left is former German president Richard von Weizsäcker. All three are honorary citizens of Gdańsk. Photograph taken at the Gdańsk celebration of Grass's 80th birthday, autumn 2007.

Grass wrote a long letter to Gdańsk Mayor
Paweł Adamowicz. Adamowicz took it to Wałęsa.
He read Grass's confession:

*(...) In the book which describes my life, (...) I recall how, in
the youthful blindness of a fifteen-year-old I volunteered to
serve on submarines, but was rejected. Instead in September
1944, when I was almost seventeen, I was involuntarily
drafted into the Waffen SS. Many from my generation
suffered a similar fate. I survived those two weeks of my
involvement in the War (...) probably only by chance. (...)
I kept to myself this episode from my young years that was
brief, but which weighed on me heavily. I did not erase
it from my memory, though. Only now, in my old age, have
I found the form to discuss it in a wider context.*

*This silence can be judged as a mistake (...), I can also be
condemned. I also have to resign myself to the fact that my
Honorary Citizenship is being put into question by many
of the people of Gdańsk. (...) I would like to keep the right to
say that I have understood this painful lesson that life taught
me when I was a young man. My books and my political
activity are the proof.*

*I am sorry that I have forced you and the people of Gdańsk,
a city with which as a Gdańsker by birth I am so closely tied,
to take a decision which would be surely easier and possibly
more justified were my book already translated into Polish.
(...)*

*When very early on, already in the early 1950s, I had
to realise that the loss of my home town resulting from
Germany's guilt was irrevocable, I publicly expressed this –
admittedly – painful fact, including in December 1970 when
I accompanied then-chancellor Willy Brandt in Warsaw.*

*Since then, thanks to Gdańsk's post-War history, this loss has
become much less painful for me, because it was from your
and my home town that the important political impulses
came in the form of a repeated eruption of workers fighting
for freedom, a movement which, later, under the name
of Solidarity, went down in history, as did its leader –
Lech Wałęsa.*

*In my books this movement found its literary reflection in my
political texts, where I indicated that Gdańsk was the first
to prevent bloodshed thanks to the Round Table. I had many
reasons to be proud of my home town, whose spirit radiated
throughout Europe, which ended a dictatorship in a non-
violent way, made a key contribution to the fall of the Berlin
wall and opened the road to true democracy.*

*All this gave me solace to resume the repeatedly stalling
dialogue between Poles and Germans, between Germans
and Poles, so that we all could learn from this lesson,
no matter how painful it might be, to better understand
each other."*

"I feel satisfied upon reading Grass's words," said
Wałęsa. "I admit that I had suspected him of
trying to use that story to publicise his book. I have
understood, however, that his story about serving in
the SS is a confession. That is why I withdraw from
any dispute with Mr Grass. I had attacked him rather
acutely for his past, but his current motives are what is
most important. It's all right, he has my forgiveness."

The meeting of the two Nobel Prize winners at the
University of Gdańsk a year later was a token of their
mutual respect. They talked there and Wałęsa shook
Grass's hand.

Gdańsk Lech Wałęsa Airport, 200 Słowackiego St.

This was the first post-war Polish airport built completely from scratch and was opened on 2 May 1974. As the third largest airport in Poland, it serves as a reserve airport for Warsaw. In the crisis-ridden communist Poland of the late 1970s there was no money to build the planned passenger and cargo terminals; therefore, the only terminal was an adapted shed. A European standard terminal was built here already in free Poland. The first passenger was cleared in the new terminal in the year of Gdańsk's millennium, on 4 August 1997. By 2012 the visitors coming to Gdańsk for the European Football Championship will be greeted by an even more modern airport.

Not only are Gdańskers flying more and more, but also more and more people are visiting Pomerania. This results from our region's tourist attractiveness and economic activity.

The city is commemorated in the name of the SPLPB Gdańsk, a Boeing 767-300 belonging to LOT, Poland's national carrier, which serves long distance flights to New York, Chicago and Toronto. Since May 1995, when it was christened Gdańsk by Danuta Wałęsa, the plane has been airborne for some 63,000 hours and has made some eight thousand landings.

Gdańsk Airport's logo is Wałęsa's sweeping signature. It is from here that he still often flies to somewhere in Europe or further abroad, where he meets with those who want to hear him personally deliver the story of the road to freedom and about the crossing of the limits of human imagination.

*"Information has also transcended borders: satellite
television, mobile communications and the Internet have
turned our world into a 'global village'. Retaining a
monopoly in such conditions is very difficult, impossible
even. The economy also does not respect borders. (...) All this
forces us to think in global, or at least continental categories."*
[MIIIRP]

And so ends our generation's most important journey by
a young incomer from Popowo to Gdańsk.

Gdańsk gave him a career as if from a Hollywood
movie. He gave Gdańsk the unforgettable memory
of participating in the development of the history
of the country, Europe and the world "live."

Gdańsk Airport has been named after L. Wałęsa since May 2004.

Postscript

The Shipyard – the penultimate scene

From this aerial journey to Europe and beyond we must, however, get back to earth: to the Gdańsk Shipyard. It fell on hard times already in the 1980s. The economic crisis in Poland overlapped with the global bear market in the shipbuilding industry. The Shipyard was still operating thanks to Soviet orders made within Comecon, the Council for Mutual Economic Assistance.

In 1988, the Shipyard found itself at a critical point. The government of Mieczysław F. Rakowski gave economic reasons for its decision to shut down the Shipyard. For the Shipyard workers and some economists, however, the decision was political.

In this terrible situation, billionaire Barbara Piasecka-Johnson, the heiress to the Johnson & Johnson fortune, came to Gdańsk in 1989.

It was a warm sunny June day. Piasecka-Johnson and Wałęsa took part in a Corpus Christi Day procession on the streets of Gdańsk.

"I will invest a hundred million dollars in the Shipyard!!!" Piasecka-Johnson declared unexpectedly. The Shipyard workers' hopes were revived. But business is business. Piasecka hired an auditing firm. The auditors went over the financial books... Half a year went by and the transaction was not made. Then, as now, no one really wants to talk about the reasons. Piasecka herself was supposed to have said then that the preparations to purchase the Shipyard cost her seven million dollars. To this day, those in the know claim that one of the appraisals of the real value of the Shipyard totalled a sum just slightly higher than that, practically worth its weight in scrap.

The Shipyard was sinking. Before it would sink, it would yet again make the world's headlines on 2 April 1996, again because of its most famous employee. Somewhere around six in the morning the former Polish President, in a black Mercedes with bodyguards in tow and surrounded by over a hundred journalists, returned in protest to his old workplace.

An electrician's wage, even for a former president, was some six million pre-denomination zlotys.

"And maintaining the house costs ten million. I don't know what my wife will say," says Wałęsa.

The Shipyard Worker's Number was the same: 61,878. His new permanent employee's pass was number 15,390. And he got a set of new screwdrivers as a gift...

Wałęsa's demonstration was due to the fact that for a long time the government could not come up with any idea of what to do with a former president who had not yet reached retirement age.

The year 1996 was symbolic for the Shipyard. On 8 June the shareholders' assembly passed a resolution to cease the Shipyard's economic activity and on 8 August, the court declared its bankruptcy. The Shipyard was sinking again. Sink it would not, as a new owner was found. But there would again be disputes and controversies, prosecutor's investigations, court suits and political brouhaha...

When speaking of the Shipyard's road out of bankruptcy then, in the latter half of the 1990s, we must absolutely emphasise the fruitlessness of the search for a serious industry investor from the Western world, which operated according to the rules of the free market. The Gdańsk Shipyard became well known in the world thanks to Solidarity, Lech Wałęsa and the non-violent struggle to overthrow communism. In a word, it was tied to great politics. But that was the very reason why many companies refused to even start preliminary negotiations. Companies from the Far East and Scandinavia were afraid to get involved in the Shipyard because they knew that it was "up to its ears" in politics. All over the world, the Shipyard was associated with Poland's fight for independence. No one belittled these merits, but at the same time no one wanted to invest in a legend. The shipbuilding business does not have a lot in common with freedom fighting.

Today, the Shipyard belongs to the Ukrainian Steel Donbas concern. And even though they are our Slavic, brotherly souls, as they say, it ain't no picnic.

The never ending Shipyard story...

Strasbourg, in front of the European Parliament

Standing here we see the national flags of the Member
States of the European Union on the masts. The 3rd
of May, 2004 was a doubly symbolic day. The flags
of the ten new Member States of the European Union,
including Poland, were run up the masts. They fluttered
on masts made in Gdańsk Shipyard. Pat Cox, the then
President of the European Parliament, hit upon
the idea.

"Gdańsk, Lech Wałęsa and the Solidarity movement
forever changed the face of Europe. There have been
few movements, few individuals who have contributed
so much to the development of freedom on our
continent. Gdańsk and the Gdańsk Shipyard workers
deserve a symbolic thank you for the events of almost
a quarter of a century ago, which helped tear down
the iron curtain and made the unification of Europe
possible," said Cox.

"Today is when the testament of the previous generation
is fulfilled," replied Wałęsa. And the struggle for
Europe was long and very costly. "The Soviet Union
and the Warsaw Pact had to fall. And the biggest
obstacles were removed by the Polish and international
Solidarity. We were able to succeed together in this
effort only because we could, when fighting, fall down
on our knees and appeal to the Divine Power."

The European Solidarity Centre

The Shipyard, the place where it all began, is dying down in a way, but at the same time it is changing. It no longer sprawls over well over 100 hectares, but takes up half of what it used to. It no longer employs well over a dozen thousand workers, as it did in the 1970s, but less than three thousand. The electric pallet trucks, which Lech Wałęsa used to repair, and which would transport not only the equipment needed in the Shipyard Departments, but also hot coffee and calls for strike, especially in December 1970 and August 1980, are hardly there anymore. This is the reality of the free market.

Recent history has hit Gdańsk and the Gdańsk Shipyard both hard and often. This is a very real social, political and economic fact, which concerns this place which is unique not only in the history of the city and Poland.

Although many historians argue that history does not repeat itself, we can say that it can come around full circle.

Centuries ago, the Teutonic Order created a suburb called the Young Town (*Jungstadt*) on this site. It lasted for less than a century, as it was torn down by the Gdańsk townspeople. For centuries the site of theYoung Town remained unused, as it was a defensive foreground for Gdańsk.

In the 19th century the shipyard of Johann Klawitter was built here, which in turn became the Imperial Shipyard and the Gdańsk Shipyard.

*On the 25th anniversary of August '80 the Founding Act of the European Solidarity Centre was
signed in front of the Shipyard. The signatories included over 20 European presidents and prime
ministers and Jose Manuel Barroso, the President of the European Commission. The photograph
shows Lech Wałęsa with his trademark pen. In the first row behind him sit: Gdańsk Mayor
Paweł Adamowicz, Solidarity Chairman Janusz Śniadek and Polish Prime Minister Marek Belka.*

W XXV rocznicę podpisania w Gdańsku Porozumień Sierpniowych,
które utorowały drogę do powstania Niezależnego Samorządnego Związku Zawodowego „Solidarność" -
pierwszej niezawisłej od reżimu komunistycznego organizacji związkowej za żelazną kurtyną,
a zarazem wielkiego ruchu obywatelskiego, który otworzył Polsce oraz narodom Europy Środkowej
i Wschodniej drogę do wolności i demokracji, a także walnie przyczynił się do prawdziwego zjednoczenia Europy,
uznając historyczną konieczność upamiętnienia przełomowej roli „Solidarności" w najnowszych dziejach Polski, Europy i świata,
niniejszym wyrażamy wolę powołania w Gdańsku Europejskiego Centrum Solidarności.

Jest naszą intencją, aby Europejskie Centrum Solidarności było instytucją łączącą funkcje
naukowe, kulturalne i edukacyjne z nowoczesną placówką muzealną oraz archiwum,
dokumentującym działania ruchów demokratycznych i wolnościowych w najnowszej historii Polski i Europy.
Pragniemy, aby ten żywy pomnik - symbol zwycięstwa pokojowej rewolucji „Solidarności" -
stanowił światowe centrum krzewienia idei wolności, demokracji i solidarności.

W obecności twórców i uczestników polskiego i gdańskiego Sierpnia '80,
znamienitych gości uroczystości rocznicowych, głów państw i szefów rządów,

AKT EREKCYJNY
EUROPEJSKIEGO CENTRUM SOLIDARNOŚCI
W GDAŃSKU
podpisują

H.E. Mr. Lech Wałęsa
First Chairman of Solidarity

H.E. Mr. Aleksander Kwaśniewski
President of the Republic of Poland

H.E. Mr. Marek Belka
Prime Minister of the Republic of Poland

Mr. Janusz Śniadek
Chairman of the National Commission of Solidarity

o czym zaświadczają

H.E. Mr. Mikheil Saakashvili
President of Georgia

H.E. Mr. László Sólyom
President of the Republic of Hungary

H.E. Mr. Boris Tadić
President of Serbia

H.E. Mr. Ivo Sander
Prime Minister of the Republic of Croatia

H.E. Mr. Jiři Paroubek
Prime Minister of the Czech Republic

H.E. Mr. Andrus Ansip
Prime Minister of the Republic of Estonia

H.E. Mr. Vlado Buckovski
Prime Minister of the Former Yugoslav Republic of Macedonia

H.E. Mr. Jan Peter Balkenende
Prime Minister of the Kingdom of Netherlands

H.E. Mr. Mikuláš Dzurinda
Prime Minister of the Slovak Republic

H.E. Mr. Markó Béla
Deputy Prime Minister of Romania

H.E. Archbishop Stanisław Dziwisz
Special Representative of the Holy See

H.E. Mr. Jacek Saryusz-Wolski
Vice President of the European Parliament

On the 25th anniversary of the signing of the August Agreements in Gdańsk,
which paved the way for the establishment of the Independent Self-Governing Trade Union Solidarity –
the first trade union organization behind the Iron Curtain independent of the communist regime,
and a great civic movement, which launched Poland and other nations of Central and Eastern Europe
on the path to freedom and democracy, and also crucially contributed to the true unification of Europe,
recognizing the need to commemorate the pivotal role of Solidarity in the contemporary history of Poland, Europe and the world,
we hereby express the will to establish the European Solidarity Center in Gdańsk.

It is our intention that the European Solidarity Center should be an institution combining research,
cultural and educational functions with those of a modern museum and archive,
documenting the achievements of democratic and freedom movements in Poland and Europe's most recent history.
We want this living monument - a symbol of the victory of Solidarity's peaceful revolution -
to become a world center for promoting the ideas of freedom, democracy and solidarity.

In the presence of the leaders and participants of the Polish and Gdańsk August '80,
distinguished guests of the commemoration ceremonies - heads of state and government,

THIS ACT FOR THE ERECTION
OF THE EUROPEAN SOLIDARITY CENTER
IN GDAŃSK

is hereby signed by

H.E. Mr. José Manuel Durão Barroso
President of the European Commission

H.E. Mr. John Prescott
For the EU Presidency
Deputy Prime Minister of the United Kingdom

Mr. Jan Kozłowski
President of Pomorskie Voivodship

Mr. Paweł Adamowicz
Mayor of the City of Gdańsk

in witness whereof

H.E. Mr. Victor Yuschenko
President of Ukraine

H.E. Mr. Guy Verhofstadt
Prime Minister of the Kingdom of Belgium

H.E. Mr. Sergei Stanishev
Prime Minister of the Republic of Bulgaria

H.E. Mr. Matti Vanhanen
Prime Minister of the Republic of Finland

H.E. Mr. Aigars Kalvitis
Prime Minister of the Republic of Latvia

H.E. Mr. Algirdas Brazauskas
Prime Minister of the Republic of Lithuania

H.E. Mr. Janez Janša
Prime Minister of the Republic of Slovenia

H.E. Mr. Göran Persson
Prime Minister of the Kingdom of Sweden

H.E. Mr. Tonio Borg
Deputy Prime Minister of the Republic of Malta

Today, when the Shipyard no longer needs so much area to build ships, it has concentrated its operation on Ostrów Island. And a new Young Town will be built in the post-Shipyard area together with the European Solidarity Centre (ESC).

The new district will retain some of the original Shipyard development considered historical monuments with the historical BHP Hall. This part of the post-Shipyard area will have housing development, modern office buildings, waterfront cafes, boutiques, hotels and cinemas. The new development will have a central traffic artery called the Promenade of Freedom, with clear symbols: the Monument to the Fallen Shipyard Workers, Gate No. 2, the ESC, BHP Hall and the pier with the bridge to Ostrów Island, opening a view on the River Martwa Wisła.

The European Solidarity Centre will stand near the historic Gate No. 2. The founding act was signed on the twenty-fifth anniversary of August. The signatories included over 20 European presidents and prime ministers and Jose Manuel Barroso, the President of the European Commission. Keen-eyed participants of the ceremony noticed, however, that German President Horst Köhler did not sign the declaration.

The silver jubilee of August in the post-Shipyard area saw the concert of electronic music legend Jean Michel Jarre. The concert was symbolically entitled *Space of Freedom*. This was much more than a concert for the largest audience in Poland. At this great multimedia spectacle over 120 thousand people could reminisce or, as young people, get to know a good bit of history which took place at this very spot.

Wałęsa said then,

Just as twenty-five years ago, the walls will come tumbling down; the walls which divide us from each other; the walls of indifference, injustice, hostility and misunderstanding. May Europe learn from Gdańsk how to build Solidarity, and all the walls will come tumbling down...

The European Solidarity Centre which will rise in this particular place must somehow answer the challenge of history, which here had the main stage for its great spectacle. This was the place where the new Gdańsk, the new Europe and the new world were born.

Electronic music legend Jean Michel Jarre gave a concert in Gdańsk on 26 August 2007 to commemorate the 25th anniversary of August '80.

Visualisation of the European Solidarity Centre building in Gdańsk, which will be erected in the post-Shipyard area. Design: Fort Studio, Gdańsk.

List of abbreviations used and their explanation

ANTY – Zbigniew Gach, *Antybohater* [Antihero], Wydawnictwo i Agencja Dziennikarzy Fopress, Wrocław 1991.

BW – An Interview with Bogdan Wałęsa, typescript from the archives of Piotr Adamowicz.

BZS – Jarosław Wąsowicz SDB, *Biało-zielona „Solidarność". O fenomenie politycznym kibiców gdańskiej Lechii 1981–1989* [The White and Green Solidarity. The Political Phenomenon of Lechia Gdańsk Supporters 1981-1989], Wydawnictwo FINNA, Gdańsk 2006.

DAK – film footage by Adam Kinaszewski, from his archives.

DdW – Lech Wałęsa, *Droga do wolności 1985–1990. Decydujące lata* [Road to Freedom 1985-1990. The Decisive Years], with Arkadiusz Rybicki, Editions Spotkania, Warszawa 1991.

DN – Lech Wałęsa, *Droga nadziei. Autobiografia* [The Road of Freedom. An Autobiography], with Andrzej Drzycimski and Adam Kinaszewski, Znak, Kraków 1989.

DW – *Historia weszła w nasze życie* [History Entered Our Lives], interview by Piotr Adamowicz with Danuta Wałęsa, *Rzeczpospolita*, 27 September 2003; *Tyle życzliwości, ile zaznałam…* [All the Kindness I've Experienced], interview by Piotr Adamowicz with Danuta Wałęsa, *Rzeczpospolita*, 13 August 2005.

FD – *Lech Wałęsa – bilans dwóch dekad* [Lech Wałęsa, an Assessment of Two Decades], documentary film, dir. Adam Kinaszewski, TVP1, 2003.

IPN – IPN Gd. 0046/ 824 t. 1, *Materiały dotyczące obserwacji Lecha Wałęsy oraz jego miejsca zamieszkania, lata 1982–1990.* [Institute of National Remembrance, Materials concerning the Surveillance of Lech Wałęsa and His Place of Residence, 1982-1990].

IKJK – Andrzej Kępiński, *Inaczej. Kto jest kim* [Another Way. Who is Who?], with Maria Jolanta Kępińska, Zbigniew Kilar, Czas, Gdańsk 1989.

JDBN – *Jeden drugiego brzemiona noście. III pielgrzymka Jana Pawła II do Ojczyzny. Gdynia – Gdańsk (dokumentacja i reportaże)* [Carry each other's burdens. The 3rd Pilgrimage of John Paul II to His Homeland. Gdynia – Gdańsk (documentary)], eds. Andrzej Drzycimski, Grzegorz Fortuna, Father Zbigniew Bryk, Gdańsk Curia, Gdańsk 1988.

MIIIRP – Lech Wałęsa, Moja III RP. *Straciłem cierpliwość* [My 3rd Polish Republic. I have Lost My Patience], with Bartosz Loba and Piotr Gulczyński, Świat Książki, Warszawa 2007.

NdW – Henryka Dobosz, Adam Kinaszewski, *Nobel dla Wałęsy* [The Nobel for Wałęsa], Libertas, Warszawa 1984.

PZM – Piotr Zaremba, *Młodopolacy. Historia Ruchu Młodej Polski* [The Young Poles. A History of the Young Poland Movement], Wydawnictwo Arche, Gdańsk 2000.

RJT – An Interview by Piotr Adamowicz with Jacek Taylor, typescript from the archives of Piotr Adamowicz.

SJH – Jerzy Holzer, *„Solidarność" 1980–1981. Geneza i historia* [Solidarity 1980-1981. Genesis and History], Wydawnictwo Krąg, Warszawa 1984.

SR – *Wspomnienia Sławomira Rybickiego* [Sławomir Rybicki Remembers], typescript from the archives of Piotr Adamowicz.

TG – *Chodziło o to, żeby pomóc narodowi* [The Idea Was to Help the Nation], an interview with Archbishop Tadeusz Gocłowski, Metropolitan of Gdańsk by Piotr Adamowicz and Ewa K. Czaczkowska, *Rzeczpospolita*, 12 April 2008.

TGA – Timothy Garton Ash, *Polska rewolucja: Solidarność* [The Polish Revolution: Solidarity], Wydawnictwo Most, Warszawa 1987.

ZRG – *Zapis rokowań gdańskich. Sierpień 1980* [Record of the Gdańsk Negotiations. August 1980], collected by Andrzej Drzycimski and Tadeusz Skutnik, Editions Spotkania, Paryż, No Date.

GDAŃSK

www.gdansk.pl

Publisher: Gdańsk City Office

Text: Piotr Adamowicz, Andrzej Drzycimski, Adam Kinaszewski

Preliminary research and selection of photographs:
Piotr Adamowicz and Andrzej Drzycimski

Editing and proof-reading: Media Profil

Photographs: Erazm Ciołek, East News, the European Solidarity Centre in Gdańsk, Kosycarz Foto Press, Mayor's Office for City Promotion at the Gdańsk City Office; and the private collections of: Bożena Rybicka-Grzywaczewska, Andrzej Kowalczys and Jarosław Rybicki

Translated by: Piotr Łuba

English proof-reading: Richard Ashcroft

Graphic design: Yellow Factory

Print: Drukarnia WL

Thanks to the Branch Office for Access and Archiving at the Institute of National Remembrance in Gdańsk, directed by Marzena Kruk; and to Grzegorz Fortune, editor-in-chief of Gdańsk monthly *30 dni*.

Thanks also to: Danuta Giecołd-Gębska, Andrzej Januszajtis, Edward Lipski – President of Elektromontaż Gdańsk S.A., Krzysztof Pusz, Krzysztof Szewczyk – Director of PKO BP S.A. Bank Branch Office No. 1 in Gdańsk, and Tomasz Tomczak – President of ZREMB FMB sp. z o.o. in Gdańsk

ISBN: 978-83-928097-1-5